THE TRAGEDY OF KING LEAR

by William Shakespeare

Contents

ACT V
Scene I. The Camp of the British Forces near Dover.
Scene II. A field between the two Camps.
Scene III. The British Camp near Dover.

Dramatis Personæ

LEAR, King of Britain.
GONERIL, eldest daughter to Lear.
REGAN, second daughter to Lear.
CORDELIA, youngest daughter to Lear.
DUKE of ALBANY, married to Goneril.
DUKE of CORNWALL, married to Regan.
KING of FRANCE.
DUKE of BURGUNDY.
EARL of GLOUCESTER.
EDGAR, elder son to Gloucester.
EDMUND, younger bastard son to Gloucester.
EARL of KENT.
FOOL.
OSWALD, steward to Goneril.
CURAN, a Courtier.
OLD MAN, Tenant to Gloucester.
Physician.
An Officer employed by Edmund.
Gentleman, attendant on Cordelia.
A Herald.
Servants to Cornwall.

Knights attending on the King, Officers, Messengers, Soldiers and Attendants.

SCENE: Britain.

ACT I

SCENE I. A Room of State in King Lear's Palace.

Enter KENT, GLOUCESTER *and* EDMUND.

KENT.
I thought the King had more affected the Duke of Albany than Cornwall.

GLOUCESTER.
It did always seem so to us; but now, in the division of the kingdom, it appears not which of the Dukes he values most, for qualities are so weighed that curiosity in neither can make choice of either's moiety.

KENT.
Is not this your son, my lord?

GLOUCESTER.
His breeding, sir, hath been at my charge: I have so often blush'd to acknowledge him that now I am braz'd to't.

KENT.
I cannot conceive you.

GLOUCESTER.
Sir, this young fellow's mother could; whereupon she grew round-wombed, and had indeed, sir, a son for her cradle ere she had a husband for her bed. Do you smell a fault?

KENT.
I cannot wish the fault undone, the issue of it being so proper.

GLOUCESTER.
But I have a son, sir, by order of law, some year elder than this, who yet is no dearer in my account: though this knave came something saucily to the world before he was sent for, yet was his mother fair; there was good sport at his making, and the whoreson must be acknowledged. Do you know this noble gentleman, Edmund?

EDMUND.
No, my lord.

GLOUCESTER.
My Lord of Kent: remember him hereafter as my honourable friend.

EDMUND.
My services to your lordship.

KENT.
I must love you, and sue to know you better.

EDMUND.
Sir, I shall study deserving.

GLOUCESTER.
He hath been out nine years, and away he shall again. The King is coming.

[*Sennet within.*]

   Enter LEAR, CORNWALL, ALBANY, GONERIL, REGAN, CORDELIA *and Attendants.*

LEAR.
Attend the lords of France and Burgundy,
Gloucester.

GLOUCESTER.
I shall, my lord.

[*Exeunt* GLOUCESTER *and* EDMUND.]

LEAR.
Meantime we shall express our darker purpose.
Give me the map there. Know that we have divided
In three our kingdom: and 'tis our fast intent
To shake all cares and business from our age;
Conferring them on younger strengths, while we
Unburden'd crawl toward death. Our son of Cornwall,
And you, our no less loving son of Albany,
We have this hour a constant will to publish
Our daughters' several dowers, that future strife
May be prevented now. The princes, France and Burgundy,
Great rivals in our youngest daughter's love,
Long in our court have made their amorous sojourn,
And here are to be answer'd. Tell me, my daughters,—
Since now we will divest us both of rule,
Interest of territory, cares of state,—
Which of you shall we say doth love us most?
That we our largest bounty may extend
Where nature doth with merit challenge.—Goneril,
Our eldest born, speak first.

GONERIL.
Sir, I love you more than word can wield the matter;
Dearer than eyesight, space, and liberty;
Beyond what can be valu'd, rich or rare;
No less than life, with grace, health, beauty, honour;
As much as child e'er lov'd, or father found;

A love that makes breath poor and speech unable;
Beyond all manner of so much I love you.

CORDELIA.
[*Aside.*] What shall Cordelia speak? Love, and be silent.

LEAR.
Of all these bounds, even from this line to this,
With shadowy forests and with champains rich'd,
With plenteous rivers and wide-skirted meads,
We make thee lady: to thine and Albany's issue
Be this perpetual.—What says our second daughter,
Our dearest Regan, wife of Cornwall? Speak.

REGAN.
Sir, I am made of the self mettle as my sister,
And prize me at her worth. In my true heart
I find she names my very deed of love;
Only she comes too short, that I profess
Myself an enemy to all other joys
Which the most precious square of sense possesses,
And find I am alone felicitate
In your dear highness' love.

CORDELIA.
[*Aside.*] Then poor Cordelia,
And yet not so; since, I am sure, my love's
More ponderous than my tongue.

LEAR.
To thee and thine hereditary ever
Remain this ample third of our fair kingdom;
No less in space, validity, and pleasure
Than that conferr'd on Goneril.—Now, our joy,
Although the last and least; to whose young love
The vines of France and milk of Burgundy
Strive to be interess'd; what can you say to draw
A third more opulent than your sisters? Speak.

CORDELIA.
Nothing, my lord.

LEAR.
Nothing?

CORDELIA.
Nothing.

LEAR.
Nothing will come of nothing: speak again.

CORDELIA.
Unhappy that I am, I cannot heave
My heart into my mouth: I love your majesty
According to my bond; no more nor less.

LEAR.
How, how, Cordelia? Mend your speech a little,
Lest you may mar your fortunes.

CORDELIA.
Good my lord,
You have begot me, bred me, lov'd me: I
Return those duties back as are right fit,
Obey you, love you, and most honour you.
Why have my sisters husbands if they say
They love you all? Haply, when I shall wed,
That lord whose hand must take my plight shall carry
Half my love with him, half my care and duty:
Sure I shall never marry like my sisters,
To love my father all.

LEAR.
But goes thy heart with this?

CORDELIA.
Ay, my good lord.

LEAR.
So young, and so untender?

CORDELIA.
So young, my lord, and true.

LEAR.
Let it be so, thy truth then be thy dower:
For, by the sacred radiance of the sun,
The mysteries of Hecate and the night;
By all the operation of the orbs,
From whom we do exist and cease to be;
Here I disclaim all my paternal care,
Propinquity and property of blood,

And as a stranger to my heart and me
Hold thee from this for ever. The barbarous Scythian,
Or he that makes his generation messes
To gorge his appetite, shall to my bosom
Be as well neighbour'd, pitied, and reliev'd,
As thou my sometime daughter.

KENT.
Good my liege,—

LEAR.
Peace, Kent!
Come not between the dragon and his wrath.
I lov'd her most, and thought to set my rest
On her kind nursery. [*To Cordelia.*] Hence and avoid my sight!
So be my grave my peace, as here I give
Her father's heart from her! Call France. Who stirs?
Call Burgundy! Cornwall and Albany,
With my two daughters' dowers digest this third:
Let pride, which she calls plainness, marry her.
I do invest you jointly with my power,
Pre-eminence, and all the large effects
That troop with majesty. Ourself, by monthly course,
With reservation of an hundred knights,
By you to be sustain'd, shall our abode
Make with you by due turn. Only we shall retain
The name, and all the addition to a king; the sway,
Revenue, execution of the rest,
Beloved sons, be yours; which to confirm,
This coronet part between you.

[*Giving the crown.*]

KENT.
Royal Lear,
Whom I have ever honour'd as my king,
Lov'd as my father, as my master follow'd,
As my great patron thought on in my prayers.—

LEAR.
The bow is bent and drawn; make from the shaft.

KENT.
Let it fall rather, though the fork invade
The region of my heart: be Kent unmannerly

When Lear is mad. What wouldst thou do, old man?
Think'st thou that duty shall have dread to speak,
When power to flattery bows? To plainness honour's bound
When majesty falls to folly. Reverse thy state;
And in thy best consideration check
This hideous rashness: answer my life my judgement,
Thy youngest daughter does not love thee least;
Nor are those empty-hearted, whose low sounds
Reverb no hollowness.

LEAR.
Kent, on thy life, no more.

KENT.
My life I never held but as a pawn
To wage against thine enemies; ne'er fear to lose it,
Thy safety being the motive.

LEAR.
Out of my sight!

KENT.
See better, Lear; and let me still remain
The true blank of thine eye.

LEAR.
Now, by Apollo,—

KENT.
Now by Apollo, King,
Thou swear'st thy gods in vain.

LEAR.
O vassal! Miscreant!

[*Laying his hand on his sword.*]

ALBANY and CORNWALL.
Dear sir, forbear!

KENT.
Kill thy physician, and the fee bestow
Upon the foul disease. Revoke thy gift,
Or, whilst I can vent clamour from my throat,
I'll tell thee thou dost evil.

LEAR.
Hear me, recreant! on thine allegiance, hear me!

Since thou hast sought to make us break our vows,
Which we durst never yet, and with strain'd pride
To come betwixt our sentences and our power,
Which nor our nature, nor our place can bear,
Our potency made good, take thy reward.
Five days we do allot thee for provision,
To shield thee from disasters of the world;
And on the sixth to turn thy hated back
Upon our kingdom: if, on the next day following,
Thy banish'd trunk be found in our dominions,
The moment is thy death. Away! By Jupiter,
This shall not be revok'd.

KENT.
Fare thee well, King: sith thus thou wilt appear,
Freedom lives hence, and banishment is here.
[*To Cordelia.*] The gods to their dear shelter take thee, maid,
That justly think'st and hast most rightly said!
[*To Goneril and Regan.*] And your large speeches may your deeds approve,
That good effects may spring from words of love.
Thus Kent, O princes, bids you all adieu;
He'll shape his old course in a country new.

[*Exit.*]

Flourish. Re-enter GLOUCESTER, *with* FRANCE, BURGUNDY *and Attendants.*

CORDELIA.
Here's France and Burgundy, my noble lord.

LEAR.
My Lord of Burgundy,
We first address toward you, who with this king
Hath rivall'd for our daughter: what in the least
Will you require in present dower with her,
Or cease your quest of love?

BURGUNDY.
Most royal majesty,
I crave no more than hath your highness offer'd,
Nor will you tender less?

LEAR.
Right noble Burgundy,
When she was dear to us, we did hold her so;
But now her price is fall'n. Sir, there she stands:

If aught within that little-seeming substance,
Or all of it, with our displeasure piec'd,
And nothing more, may fitly like your grace,
She's there, and she is yours.

BURGUNDY.
I know no answer.

LEAR.
Will you, with those infirmities she owes,
Unfriended, new adopted to our hate,
Dower'd with our curse, and stranger'd with our oath,
Take her or leave her?

BURGUNDY.
Pardon me, royal sir;
Election makes not up in such conditions.

LEAR.
Then leave her, sir; for, by the power that made me,
I tell you all her wealth. [*To France*] For you, great king,
I would not from your love make such a stray
To match you where I hate; therefore beseech you
T'avert your liking a more worthier way
Than on a wretch whom nature is asham'd
Almost t'acknowledge hers.

FRANCE.
This is most strange,
That she, who even but now was your best object,
The argument of your praise, balm of your age,
The best, the dearest, should in this trice of time
Commit a thing so monstrous, to dismantle
So many folds of favour. Sure her offence
Must be of such unnatural degree
That monsters it, or your fore-vouch'd affection
Fall into taint; which to believe of her
Must be a faith that reason without miracle
Should never plant in me.

CORDELIA.
I yet beseech your majesty,
If for I want that glib and oily art
To speak and purpose not; since what I well intend,
I'll do't before I speak,—that you make known

It is no vicious blot, murder, or foulness,
No unchaste action or dishonour'd step,
That hath depriv'd me of your grace and favour;
But even for want of that for which I am richer,
A still soliciting eye, and such a tongue
As I am glad I have not, though not to have it
Hath lost me in your liking.

LEAR.
Better thou hadst
Not been born than not to have pleas'd me better.

FRANCE.
Is it but this?—a tardiness in nature
Which often leaves the history unspoke
That it intends to do? My lord of Burgundy,
What say you to the lady? Love's not love
When it is mingled with regards that stands
Aloof from the entire point. Will you have her?
She is herself a dowry.

BURGUNDY.
Royal King,
Give but that portion which yourself propos'd,
And here I take Cordelia by the hand,
Duchess of Burgundy.

LEAR.
Nothing: I have sworn; I am firm.

BURGUNDY.
I am sorry, then, you have so lost a father
That you must lose a husband.

CORDELIA.
Peace be with Burgundy!
Since that respects of fortunes are his love,
I shall not be his wife.

FRANCE.
Fairest Cordelia, that art most rich, being poor;
Most choice forsaken; and most lov'd, despis'd!
Thee and thy virtues here I seize upon:
Be it lawful, I take up what's cast away.
Gods, gods! 'Tis strange that from their cold'st neglect
My love should kindle to inflam'd respect.

Thy dowerless daughter, King, thrown to my chance,
Is queen of us, of ours, and our fair France:
Not all the dukes of waterish Burgundy
Can buy this unpriz'd precious maid of me.
Bid them farewell, Cordelia, though unkind:
Thou losest here, a better where to find.

LEAR.
Thou hast her, France: let her be thine; for we
Have no such daughter, nor shall ever see
That face of hers again. Therefore be gone ·
Without our grace, our love, our benison.
Come, noble Burgundy.

[*Flourish. Exeunt* LEAR, BURGUNDY, CORNWALL, ALBANY, GLOUCESTER *and Attendants.*]

FRANCE.
Bid farewell to your sisters.

CORDELIA.
The jewels of our father, with wash'd eyes
Cordelia leaves you: I know you what you are;
And like a sister am most loath to call
Your faults as they are nam'd. Love well our father:
To your professed bosoms I commit him:
But yet, alas, stood I within his grace,
I would prefer him to a better place.
So farewell to you both.

REGAN.
Prescribe not us our duties.

GONERIL.
Let your study
Be to content your lord, who hath receiv'd you
At fortune's alms. You have obedience scanted,
And well are worth the want that you have wanted.

CORDELIA.
Time shall unfold what plighted cunning hides:
Who covers faults, at last shame derides.
Well may you prosper.

FRANCE.
Come, my fair Cordelia.

[*Exeunt* FRANCE *and* CORDELIA.]

GONERIL.
Sister, it is not little I have to say of what most nearly appertains to us both. I think our father will hence tonight.

REGAN.
That's most certain, and with you; next month with us.

GONERIL.
You see how full of changes his age is; the observation we have made of it hath not been little: he always loved our sister most; and with what poor judgement he hath now cast her off appears too grossly.

REGAN.
'Tis the infirmity of his age: yet he hath ever but slenderly known himself.

GONERIL.
The best and soundest of his time hath been but rash; then must we look from his age to receive not alone the imperfections of long-engrafted condition, but therewithal the unruly waywardness that infirm and choleric years bring with them.

REGAN.
Such unconstant starts are we like to have from him as this of Kent's banishment.

GONERIL.
There is further compliment of leave-taking between France and him. Pray you let us hit together: if our father carry authority with such disposition as he bears, this last surrender of his will but offend us.

REGAN.
We shall further think of it.

GONERIL.
We must do something, and i' th' heat.

[*Exeunt.*]

SCENE II. A Hall in the Earl of Gloucester's Castle.

Enter EDMUND *with a letter.*

EDMUND.
Thou, Nature, art my goddess; to thy law
My services are bound. Wherefore should I
Stand in the plague of custom, and permit
The curiosity of nations to deprive me?
For that I am some twelve or fourteen moonshines
Lag of a brother? Why bastard? Wherefore base?

When my dimensions are as well compact,
My mind as generous, and my shape as true
As honest madam's issue? Why brand they us
With base? With baseness? bastardy? Base, base?
Who, in the lusty stealth of nature, take
More composition and fierce quality
Than doth within a dull stale tired bed
Go to the creating a whole tribe of fops
Got 'tween asleep and wake? Well then,
Legitimate Edgar, I must have your land:
Our father's love is to the bastard Edmund
As to the legitimate: fine word: legitimate!
Well, my legitimate, if this letter speed,
And my invention thrive, Edmund the base
Shall top the legitimate. I grow, I prosper.
Now, gods, stand up for bastards!

Enter GLOUCESTER.

GLOUCESTER.
Kent banish'd thus! and France in choler parted!
And the King gone tonight! Prescrib'd his pow'r!
Confin'd to exhibition! All this done
Upon the gad!—Edmund, how now! What news?

EDMUND.
So please your lordship, none.

[*Putting up the letter.*]

GLOUCESTER.
Why so earnestly seek you to put up that letter?

EDMUND.
I know no news, my lord.

GLOUCESTER.
What paper were you reading?

EDMUND.
Nothing, my lord.

GLOUCESTER.
No? What needed then that terrible dispatch of it into your pocket? The quality of nothing hath not such need to hide itself. Let's see. Come, if it be nothing, I shall not need spectacles.

EDMUND.
I beseech you, sir, pardon me. It is a letter from my brother that I have not all o'er-read; and for so much as I have perus'd, I find it not fit for your o'er-looking.

GLOUCESTER.
Give me the letter, sir.

EDMUND.
I shall offend, either to detain or give it. The contents, as in part I understand them, are to blame.

GLOUCESTER.
Let's see, let's see!

EDMUND.
I hope, for my brother's justification, he wrote this but as an essay, or taste of my virtue.

GLOUCESTER.
[*Reads.*] 'This policy and reverence of age makes the world bitter to the best of our times; keeps our fortunes from us till our oldness cannot relish them. I begin to find an idle and fond bondage in the oppression of aged tyranny; who sways not as it hath power, but as it is suffered. Come to me, that of this I may speak more. If our father would sleep till I waked him, you should enjoy half his revenue for ever, and live the beloved of your brother EDGAR.'
Hum! Conspiracy? 'Sleep till I wake him, you should enjoy half his revenue.'—My son Edgar! Had he a hand to write this? A heart and brain to breed it in? When came this to you? Who brought it?

EDMUND.
It was not brought me, my lord, there's the cunning of it. I found it thrown in at the casement of my closet.

GLOUCESTER.
You know the character to be your brother's?

EDMUND.
If the matter were good, my lord, I durst swear it were his; but in respect of that, I would fain think it were not.

GLOUCESTER.
It is his.

EDMUND.
It is his hand, my lord; but I hope his heart is not in the contents.

GLOUCESTER.
Has he never before sounded you in this business?

EDMUND.
Never, my lord. But I have heard him oft maintain it to be fit that, sons at perfect age, and fathers declined, the father should be as ward to the son, and the son manage his revenue.

GLOUCESTER.
O villain, villain! His very opinion in the letter! Abhorred villain! Unnatural, detested, brutish villain! worse than brutish! Go, sirrah, seek him; I'll apprehend him. Abominable villain, Where is he?

EDMUND.
I do not well know, my lord. If it shall please you to suspend your indignation against my brother till you can derive from him better testimony of his intent, you should run a certain course; where, if you violently proceed against him, mistaking his purpose, it would make a great gap in your own honour, and shake in pieces the heart of his obedience. I dare pawn down my life for him, that he hath writ this to feel my affection to your honour, and to no other pretence of danger.

GLOUCESTER.
Think you so?

EDMUND.
If your honour judge it meet, I will place you where you shall hear us confer of this, and by an auricular assurance have your satisfaction, and that without any further delay than this very evening.

GLOUCESTER.
He cannot be such a monster.

EDMUND.
Nor is not, sure.

GLOUCESTER.
To his father, that so tenderly and entirely loves him. Heaven and earth! Edmund, seek him out; wind me into him, I pray you: frame the business after your own wisdom. I would unstate myself to be in a due resolution.

EDMUND.
I will seek him, sir, presently; convey the business as I shall find means, and acquaint you withal.

GLOUCESTER.
These late eclipses in the sun and moon portend no good to us: though the wisdom of Nature can reason it thus and thus, yet nature finds itself scourged by the sequent effects. Love cools, friendship falls off, brothers divide: in cities, mutinies; in countries, discord; in palaces, treason; and the bond cracked 'twixt son and father. This villain of mine comes under the prediction; there's son against father: the King

falls from bias of nature; there's father against child. We have seen the best of our time. Machinations, hollowness, treachery, and all ruinous disorders follow us disquietly to our graves. Find out this villain, Edmund; it shall lose thee nothing; do it carefully.—And the noble and true-hearted Kent banished! his offence, honesty! 'Tis strange.

[*Exit.*]

EDMUND.
This is the excellent foppery of the world, that, when we are sick in fortune, often the surfeits of our own behaviour, we make guilty of our disasters the sun, the moon, and the stars; as if we were villains on necessity; fools by heavenly compulsion; knaves, thieves, and treachers by spherical predominance; drunkards, liars, and adulterers by an enforced obedience of planetary influence; and all that we are evil in, by a divine thrusting on. An admirable evasion of whoremaster man, to lay his goatish disposition to the charge of a star. My father compounded with my mother under the dragon's tail, and my nativity was under Ursa Major, so that it follows I am rough and lecherous. Fut! I should have been that I am, had the maidenliest star in the firmament twinkled on my bastardizing.

   Enter EDGAR.

Pat! he comes, like the catastrophe of the old comedy: my cue is villainous melancholy, with a sigh like Tom o'Bedlam.—O, these eclipses do portend these divisions! Fa, sol, la, mi.

EDGAR.
How now, brother Edmund, what serious contemplation are you in?

EDMUND.
I am thinking, brother, of a prediction I read this other day, what should follow these eclipses.

EDGAR.
Do you busy yourself with that?

EDMUND.
I promise you, the effects he writes of succeed unhappily: as of unnaturalness between the child and the parent; death, dearth, dissolutions of ancient amities; divisions in state, menaces and maledictions against King and nobles; needless diffidences, banishment of friends, dissipation of cohorts, nuptial breaches, and I know not what.

EDGAR.
How long have you been a sectary astronomical?

EDMUND.
Come, come! when saw you my father last?

EDGAR.
The night gone by.

EDMUND.
Spake you with him?

EDGAR.
Ay, two hours together.

EDMUND.
Parted you in good terms? Found you no displeasure in him, by word nor countenance?

EDGAR.
None at all.

EDMUND.
Bethink yourself wherein you may have offended him: and at my entreaty forbear his presence until some little time hath qualified the heat of his displeasure; which at this instant so rageth in him that with the mischief of your person it would scarcely allay.

EDGAR.
Some villain hath done me wrong.

EDMUND.
That's my fear. I pray you have a continent forbearance till the speed of his rage goes slower; and, as I say, retire with me to my lodging, from whence I will fitly bring you to hear my lord speak: pray ye, go; there's my key. If you do stir abroad, go armed.

EDGAR.
Armed, brother?

EDMUND.
Brother, I advise you to the best; I am no honest man if there be any good meaning toward you: I have told you what I have seen and heard. But faintly; nothing like the image and horror of it: pray you, away!

EDGAR.
Shall I hear from you anon?

EDMUND.
I do serve you in this business.

[*Exit* EDGAR.]

A credulous father! and a brother noble,
Whose nature is so far from doing harms
That he suspects none; on whose foolish honesty
My practices ride easy! I see the business.

Let me, if not by birth, have lands by wit;
All with me's meet that I can fashion fit.

[*Exit.*]

SCENE III. A Room in the Duke of Albany's Palace.

Enter GONERIL *and* OSWALD.

GONERIL.
Did my father strike my gentleman for chiding of his fool?

OSWALD.
Ay, madam.

GONERIL.
By day and night, he wrongs me; every hour
He flashes into one gross crime or other,
That sets us all at odds; I'll not endure it:
His knights grow riotous, and himself upbraids us
On every trifle. When he returns from hunting,
I will not speak with him; say I am sick.
If you come slack of former services,
You shall do well; the fault of it I'll answer.

[*Horns within.*]

OSWALD.
He's coming, madam; I hear him.

GONERIL.
Put on what weary negligence you please,
You and your fellows; I'd have it come to question:
If he distaste it, let him to our sister,
Whose mind and mine, I know, in that are one,
Not to be overruled. Idle old man,
That still would manage those authorities
That he hath given away! Now, by my life,
Old fools are babes again; and must be us'd
With checks as flatteries, when they are seen abus'd.
Remember what I have said.

OSWALD.
Very well, madam.

GONERIL.
And let his knights have colder looks among you;
What grows of it, no matter; advise your fellows so;

I would breed from hence occasions, and I shall,
That I may speak. I'll write straight to my sister
To hold my very course. Prepare for dinner.

[*Exeunt.*]

SCENE IV. A Hall in Albany's Palace.

Enter KENT, *disguised.*

KENT.
If but as well I other accents borrow,
That can my speech defuse, my good intent
May carry through itself to that full issue
For which I rais'd my likeness. Now, banish'd Kent,
If thou canst serve where thou dost stand condemn'd,
So may it come, thy master, whom thou lov'st,
Shall find thee full of labours.

Horns within. Enter KING LEAR, *Knights and Attendants.*

LEAR.
Let me not stay a jot for dinner; go get it ready.

[*Exit an Attendant.*]

How now! what art thou?

KENT.
A man, sir.

LEAR.
What dost thou profess? What wouldst thou with us?

KENT.
I do profess to be no less than I seem; to serve him truly that will put me in trust; to love him that is honest; to converse with him that is wise and says little; to fear judgement; to fight when I cannot choose; and to eat no fish.

LEAR.
What art thou?

KENT.
A very honest-hearted fellow, and as poor as the King.

LEAR.
If thou be'st as poor for a subject as he's for a king, thou art poor enough. What wouldst thou?

KENT.
Service.

LEAR.
Who wouldst thou serve?

KENT.
You.

LEAR.
Dost thou know me, fellow?

KENT.
No, sir; but you have that in your countenance which I would fain call master.

LEAR.
What's that?

KENT.
Authority.

LEAR.
What services canst thou do?

KENT.
I can keep honest counsel, ride, run, mar a curious tale in telling it and deliver a plain message bluntly. That which ordinary men are fit for, I am qualified in, and the best of me is diligence.

LEAR.
How old art thou?

KENT.
Not so young, sir, to love a woman for singing; nor so old to dote on her for anything: I have years on my back forty-eight.

LEAR.
Follow me; thou shalt serve me. If I like thee no worse after dinner, I will not part from thee yet. Dinner, ho, dinner! Where's my knave? my fool? Go you and call my fool hither.

[*Exit an Attendant.*]

   Enter OSWALD.

You, you, sirrah, where's my daughter?

OSWALD.
So please you,—

[*Exit.*]

LEAR.
What says the fellow there? Call the clotpoll back.

[*Exit a Knight.*]

Where's my fool? Ho, I think the world's asleep.

  Re-enter KNIGHT.

How now! where's that mongrel?

KNIGHT.
He says, my lord, your daughter is not well.

LEAR.
Why came not the slave back to me when I called him?

KNIGHT.
Sir, he answered me in the roundest manner, he would not.

LEAR.
He would not?

KNIGHT.
My lord, I know not what the matter is; but to my judgement your highness is not
entertained with that ceremonious affection as you were wont; there's a great
abatement of kindness appears as well in the general dependants as in the Duke
himself also, and your daughter.

LEAR.
Ha! say'st thou so?

KNIGHT.
I beseech you pardon me, my lord, if I be mistaken; for my duty cannot be silent when
I think your highness wronged.

LEAR.
Thou but rememberest me of mine own conception: I have perceived a most faint
neglect of late; which I have rather blamed as mine own jealous curiosity than as a
very pretence and purpose of unkindness: I will look further into't. But where's my
fool? I have not seen him this two days.

KNIGHT.
Since my young lady's going into France, sir, the fool hath much pined away.

LEAR.
No more of that; I have noted it well. Go you and tell my daughter I would speak with
her.

[*Exit Attendant.*]

Go you, call hither my fool.

[Exit another Attendant.]

 Re-enter OSWALD.

O, you, sir, you, come you hither, sir: who am I, sir?

OSWALD.
My lady's father.

LEAR.
My lady's father! my lord's knave: you whoreson dog! you slave! you cur!

OSWALD.
I am none of these, my lord; I beseech your pardon.

LEAR.
Do you bandy looks with me, you rascal?

[Striking him.]

OSWALD.
I'll not be struck, my lord.

KENT.
Nor tripp'd neither, you base football player.

[Tripping up his heels.]

LEAR.
I thank thee, fellow. Thou serv'st me, and I'll love thee.

KENT.
Come, sir, arise, away! I'll teach you differences: away, away! If you will measure your lubber's length again, tarry; but away! go to; have you wisdom? So.

[Pushes OSWALD *out.]*

LEAR.
Now, my friendly knave, I thank thee: there's earnest of thy service.

[Giving KENT *money.]*

 Enter FOOL.

FOOL.
Let me hire him too; here's my coxcomb.

[Giving KENT *his cap.]*

LEAR.
How now, my pretty knave, how dost thou?

FOOL.
Sirrah, you were best take my coxcomb.

KENT.
Why, fool?

FOOL.
Why, for taking one's part that's out of favour. Nay, an thou canst not smile as the wind sits, thou'lt catch cold shortly: there, take my coxcomb: why, this fellow has banish'd two on's daughters, and did the third a blessing against his will; if thou follow him, thou must needs wear my coxcomb. How now, nuncle! Would I had two coxcombs and two daughters!

LEAR.
Why, my boy?

FOOL.
If I gave them all my living, I'd keep my coxcombs myself. There's mine; beg another of thy daughters.

LEAR.
Take heed, sirrah, the whip.

FOOL.
Truth's a dog must to kennel; he must be whipped out, when the Lady Brach may stand by the fire and stink.

LEAR.
A pestilent gall to me!

FOOL.
Sirrah, I'll teach thee a speech.

LEAR.
Do.

FOOL.
Mark it, nuncle:
    Have more than thou showest,
    Speak less than thou knowest,
    Lend less than thou owest,
    Ride more than thou goest,
    Learn more than thou trowest,
    Set less than thou throwest;
    Leave thy drink and thy whore,
    And keep in-a-door,

And thou shalt have more
Than two tens to a score.

KENT.
This is nothing, fool.

FOOL.
Then 'tis like the breath of an unfee'd lawyer, you gave me nothing for't. Can you make no use of nothing, nuncle?

LEAR.
Why, no, boy; nothing can be made out of nothing.

FOOL.
[*to Kent.*] Prythee tell him, so much the rent of his land comes to: he will not believe a fool.

LEAR.
A bitter fool.

FOOL.
Dost thou know the difference, my boy, between a bitter fool and a sweet one?

LEAR.
No, lad; teach me.

FOOL.
　That lord that counsell'd thee
　　To give away thy land,
　Come place him here by me,
　　Do thou for him stand.
　The sweet and bitter fool
　　Will presently appear;
　The one in motley here,
　　The other found out there.

LEAR.
Dost thou call me fool, boy?

FOOL.
All thy other titles thou hast given away; that thou wast born with.

KENT.
This is not altogether fool, my lord.

FOOL.
No, faith; lords and great men will not let me; if I had a monopoly out, they would have part on't and ladies too, they will not let me have all the fool to myself; they'll be snatching. Nuncle, give me an egg, and I'll give thee two crowns.

LEAR.

What two crowns shall they be?

FOOL.

Why, after I have cut the egg i' the middle and eat up the meat, the two crowns of the egg. When thou clovest thy crown i' the middle and gav'st away both parts, thou bor'st thine ass on thy back o'er the dirt: thou hadst little wit in thy bald crown when thou gav'st thy golden one away. If I speak like myself in this, let him be whipped that first finds it so.

[*Singing.*]
    Fools had ne'er less grace in a year;
       For wise men are grown foppish,
    And know not how their wits to wear,
       Their manners are so apish.

LEAR.

When were you wont to be so full of songs, sirrah?

FOOL.

I have used it, nuncle, e'er since thou mad'st thy daughters thy mothers; for when thou gav'st them the rod, and put'st down thine own breeches,

[*Singing.*]
    Then they for sudden joy did weep,
       And I for sorrow sung,
    That such a king should play bo-peep,
       And go the fools among.

Prythee, nuncle, keep a schoolmaster that can teach thy fool to lie; I would fain learn to lie.

LEAR.

An you lie, sirrah, we'll have you whipped.

FOOL.

I marvel what kin thou and thy daughters are: they'll have me whipped for speaking true; thou'lt have me whipped for lying; and sometimes I am whipped for holding my peace. I had rather be any kind o'thing than a fool: and yet I would not be thee, nuncle: thou hast pared thy wit o'both sides, and left nothing i' the middle: here comes one o' the parings.

    Enter GONERIL.

LEAR.

How now, daughter? What makes that frontlet on? Methinks you are too much of late i' the frown.

FOOL.

Thou wast a pretty fellow when thou hadst no need to care for her frowning. Now thou art an O without a figure: I am better than thou art now. I am a fool, thou art nothing. [*To Goneril.*] Yes, forsooth, I will hold my tongue. So your face bids me, though you say nothing. Mum, mum,

> He that keeps nor crust nor crum,
> Weary of all, shall want some.

[*Pointing to Lear.*] That's a shealed peascod.

GONERIL.

Not only, sir, this your all-licens'd fool,
But other of your insolent retinue
Do hourly carp and quarrel; breaking forth
In rank and not-to-be-endured riots. Sir,
I had thought, by making this well known unto you,
To have found a safe redress; but now grow fearful,
By what yourself too late have spoke and done,
That you protect this course, and put it on
By your allowance; which if you should, the fault
Would not scape censure, nor the redresses sleep,
Which, in the tender of a wholesome weal,
Might in their working do you that offence
Which else were shame, that then necessity
Will call discreet proceeding.

FOOL.

For you know, nuncle,

> The hedge-sparrow fed the cuckoo so long
> That it's had it head bit off by it young.

So out went the candle, and we were left darkling.

LEAR.

Are you our daughter?

GONERIL.

Come, sir,
I would you would make use of that good wisdom,
Whereof I know you are fraught; and put away
These dispositions, which of late transform you
From what you rightly are.

FOOL.

May not an ass know when the cart draws the horse? Whoop, Jug! I love thee!

LEAR.
Doth any here know me? This is not Lear;
Doth Lear walk thus? speak thus? Where are his eyes?
Either his notion weakens, his discernings
Are lethargied. Ha! waking? 'Tis not so!
Who is it that can tell me who I am?

FOOL.
Lear's shadow.

LEAR.
I would learn that; for by the marks of sovereignty, knowledge and reason, I should be
false persuaded I had daughters.

FOOL.
Which they will make an obedient father.

LEAR.
Your name, fair gentlewoman?

GONERIL.
This admiration, sir, is much o' the favour
Of other your new pranks. I do beseech you
To understand my purposes aright:
As you are old and reverend, you should be wise.
Here do you keep a hundred knights and squires;
Men so disorder'd, so debosh'd and bold
That this our court, infected with their manners,
Shows like a riotous inn. Epicurism and lust
Makes it more like a tavern or a brothel
Than a grac'd palace. The shame itself doth speak
For instant remedy. Be, then, desir'd
By her that else will take the thing she begs
A little to disquantity your train;
And the remainder that shall still depend,
To be such men as may besort your age,
Which know themselves, and you.

LEAR.
Darkness and devils!
Saddle my horses; call my train together.
Degenerate bastard! I'll not trouble thee:
Yet have I left a daughter.

GONERIL.
You strike my people; and your disorder'd rabble
Make servants of their betters.

Enter ALBANY.

LEAR.
Woe that too late repents!—
[*To Albany.*] O, sir, are you come?
Is it your will? Speak, sir.—Prepare my horses.
Ingratitude, thou marble-hearted fiend,
More hideous when thou show'st thee in a child
Than the sea-monster!

ALBANY.
Pray, sir, be patient.

LEAR.
[*to Goneril.*] Detested kite, thou liest.
My train are men of choice and rarest parts,
That all particulars of duty know;
And in the most exact regard support
The worships of their name. O most small fault,
How ugly didst thou in Cordelia show!
Which, like an engine, wrench'd my frame of nature
From the fix'd place; drew from my heart all love,
And added to the gall. O Lear, Lear, Lear!
[*Striking his head.*] Beat at this gate that let thy folly in
And thy dear judgement out! Go, go, my people.

ALBANY.
My lord, I am guiltless, as I am ignorant
Of what hath moved you.

LEAR.
It may be so, my lord.
Hear, nature, hear; dear goddess, hear
Suspend thy purpose, if thou didst intend
To make this creature fruitful!
Into her womb convey sterility!
Dry up in her the organs of increase;
And from her derogate body never spring
A babe to honour her! If she must teem,
Create her child of spleen, that it may live
And be a thwart disnatur'd torment to her!

Let it stamp wrinkles in her brow of youth;
With cadent tears fret channels in her cheeks;
Turn all her mother's pains and benefits
To laughter and contempt; that she may feel
How sharper than a serpent's tooth it is
To have a thankless child! Away, away!

[*Exit.*]

ALBANY.
Now, gods that we adore, whereof comes this?

GONERIL.
Never afflict yourself to know more of it;
But let his disposition have that scope
That dotage gives it.

    Re-enter LEAR.

LEAR.
What, fifty of my followers at a clap?
Within a fortnight?

ALBANY.
What's the matter, sir?

LEAR.
I'll tell thee. [*To Goneril.*] Life and death! I am asham'd
That thou hast power to shake my manhood thus;
That these hot tears, which break from me perforce,
Should make thee worth them. Blasts and fogs upon thee!
Th'untented woundings of a father's curse
Pierce every sense about thee! Old fond eyes,
Beweep this cause again, I'll pluck ye out,
And cast you with the waters that you lose
To temper clay. Ha! Let it be so.
I have another daughter,
Who, I am sure, is kind and comfortable:
When she shall hear this of thee, with her nails
She'll flay thy wolvish visage. Thou shalt find
That I'll resume the shape which thou dost think
I have cast off for ever.

[*Exeunt* LEAR, KENT *and Attendants.*]

GONERIL.
Do you mark that?

ALBANY.
I cannot be so partial, Goneril,
To the great love I bear you,—

GONERIL.
Pray you, content. What, Oswald, ho!
[*To the Fool.*] You, sir, more knave than fool, after your master.

FOOL.
Nuncle Lear, nuncle Lear, tarry and take the fool with thee.
  A fox when one has caught her,
  And such a daughter,
  Should sure to the slaughter,
  If my cap would buy a halter;
  So the fool follows after.

[*Exit.*]

GONERIL.
This man hath had good counsel.—A hundred knights!
'Tis politic and safe to let him keep
At point a hundred knights: yes, that on every dream,
Each buzz, each fancy, each complaint, dislike,
He may enguard his dotage with their powers,
And hold our lives in mercy. Oswald, I say!

ALBANY.
Well, you may fear too far.

GONERIL.
Safer than trust too far:
Let me still take away the harms I fear,
Not fear still to be taken: I know his heart.
What he hath utter'd I have writ my sister:
If she sustain him and his hundred knights,
When I have show'd th'unfitness,—

  Re-enter OSWALD.

How now, Oswald!
What, have you writ that letter to my sister?

OSWALD.
Ay, madam.

GONERIL.
Take you some company, and away to horse:

Inform her full of my particular fear;
And thereto add such reasons of your own
As may compact it more. Get you gone;
And hasten your return.

[*Exit* OSWALD.]

No, no, my lord!
This milky gentleness and course of yours,
Though I condemn not, yet, under pardon,
You are much more attask'd for want of wisdom
Than prais'd for harmful mildness.

ALBANY.
How far your eyes may pierce I cannot tell:
Striving to better, oft we mar what's well.

GONERIL.
Nay then,—

ALBANY.
Well, well; the event.

[*Exeunt.*]

SCENE V. Court before the Duke of Albany's Palace.

Enter LEAR, KENT *and* FOOL.

LEAR.
Go you before to Gloucester with these letters: acquaint my daughter no further with anything you know than comes from her demand out of the letter. If your diligence be not speedy, I shall be there afore you.

KENT.
I will not sleep, my lord, till I have delivered your letter.

[*Exit.*]

FOOL.
If a man's brains were in's heels, were't not in danger of kibes?

LEAR.
Ay, boy.

FOOL.
Then I prythee be merry; thy wit shall not go slipshod.

LEAR.
Ha, ha, ha!

FOOL.
Shalt see thy other daughter will use thee kindly, for though she's as like this as a crab's like an apple, yet I can tell what I can tell.

LEAR.
What canst tell, boy?

FOOL.
She'll taste as like this as a crab does to a crab. Thou canst tell why one's nose stands i'the middle on's face?

LEAR.
No.

FOOL.
Why, to keep one's eyes of either side's nose, that what a man cannot smell out, he may spy into.

LEAR.
I did her wrong.

FOOL.
Canst tell how an oyster makes his shell?

LEAR.
No.

FOOL.
Nor I neither; but I can tell why a snail has a house.

LEAR.
Why?

FOOL.
Why, to put's head in; not to give it away to his daughters, and leave his horns without a case.

LEAR.
I will forget my nature. So kind a father! Be my horses ready?

FOOL.
Thy asses are gone about 'em. The reason why the seven stars are no more than seven is a pretty reason.

LEAR.
Because they are not eight?

FOOL.
Yes indeed: thou wouldst make a good fool.

LEAR.
To tak't again perforce!—Monster ingratitude!

FOOL.
If thou wert my fool, nuncle, I'ld have thee beaten for being old before thy time.

LEAR.
How's that?

FOOL.
Thou shouldst not have been old till thou hadst been wise.

LEAR.
O, let me not be mad, not mad, sweet heaven!
Keep me in temper; I would not be mad!

    Enter GENTLEMAN.

How now? are the horses ready?

GENTLEMAN.
Ready, my lord.

LEAR.
Come, boy.

FOOL.
She that's a maid now, and laughs at my departure,
Shall not be a maid long, unless things be cut shorter.

[*Exeunt.*]

ACT II

SCENE I. A court within the Castle of the Earl of Gloucester.

    Enter EDMUND *and* CURAN, *meeting.*

EDMUND.
Save thee, Curan.

CURAN.
And you, sir. I have been with your father, and given him notice that the Duke of Cornwall and Regan his Duchess will be here with him this night.

EDMUND.
How comes that?

CURAN.
Nay, I know not. You have heard of the news abroad; I mean the whispered ones, for they are yet but ear-kissing arguments?

EDMUND.
Not I: pray you, what are they?

CURAN.
Have you heard of no likely wars toward, 'twixt the two dukes of Cornwall and Albany?

EDMUND.
Not a word.

CURAN.
You may do, then, in time. Fare you well, sir.

[*Exit.*]

EDMUND.
The Duke be here tonight? The better! best!
This weaves itself perforce into my business.
My father hath set guard to take my brother;
And I have one thing, of a queasy question,
Which I must act. Briefness and fortune work!
Brother, a word, descend, brother, I say!

    Enter EDGAR.

My father watches: O sir, fly this place;
Intelligence is given where you are hid;
You have now the good advantage of the night.
Have you not spoken 'gainst the Duke of Cornwall?
He's coming hither; now, i' the night, i' the haste,
And Regan with him: have you nothing said
Upon his party 'gainst the Duke of Albany?
Advise yourself.

EDGAR.
I am sure on't, not a word.

EDMUND.
I hear my father coming:—pardon me;
In cunning I must draw my sword upon you:
Draw: seem to defend yourself: now quit you well.

Yield: come before my father. Light, ho, here!
Fly, brother. Torches, torches!—So farewell.

[*Exit* EDGAR.]

Some blood drawn on me would beget opinion
Of my more fierce endeavour: [*Wounds his arm.*]
I have seen drunkards
Do more than this in sport. Father, father!
Stop, stop! No help?

    Enter GLOUCESTER *and Servants with torches.*

GLOUCESTER.
Now, Edmund, where's the villain?

EDMUND.
Here stood he in the dark, his sharp sword out,
Mumbling of wicked charms, conjuring the moon
To stand auspicious mistress.

GLOUCESTER.
But where is he?

EDMUND.
Look, sir, I bleed.

GLOUCESTER.
Where is the villain, Edmund?

EDMUND.
Fled this way, sir. When by no means he could,—

GLOUCESTER.
Pursue him, ho! Go after.

[*Exeunt Servants.*]

—By no means what?

EDMUND.
Persuade me to the murder of your lordship;
But that I told him the revenging gods
'Gainst parricides did all their thunders bend;
Spoke with how manifold and strong a bond
The child was bound to the father; sir, in fine,
Seeing how loathly opposite I stood
To his unnatural purpose, in fell motion
With his prepared sword, he charges home

My unprovided body, latch'd mine arm;
But when he saw my best alarum'd spirits,
Bold in the quarrel's right, rous'd to th'encounter,
Or whether gasted by the noise I made,
Full suddenly he fled.

GLOUCESTER.
Let him fly far;
Not in this land shall he remain uncaught;
And found—dispatch'd. The noble Duke my master,
My worthy arch and patron, comes tonight:
By his authority I will proclaim it,
That he which finds him shall deserve our thanks,
Bringing the murderous coward to the stake;
He that conceals him, death.

EDMUND.
When I dissuaded him from his intent,
And found him pight to do it, with curst speech
I threaten'd to discover him: he replied,
'Thou unpossessing bastard! dost thou think,
If I would stand against thee, would the reposal
Of any trust, virtue, or worth in thee
Make thy words faith'd? No: what I should deny
As this I would; ay, though thou didst produce
My very character, I'd turn it all
To thy suggestion, plot, and damned practice:
And thou must make a dullard of the world,
If they not thought the profits of my death
Were very pregnant and potential spurs
To make thee seek it.

GLOUCESTER.
O strange and fast'ned villain!
Would he deny his letter, said he? I never got him.

[*Tucket within.*]

Hark, the Duke's trumpets! I know not why he comes.
All ports I'll bar; the villain shall not scape;
The Duke must grant me that: besides, his picture
I will send far and near, that all the kingdom
May have due note of him; and of my land,

Loyal and natural boy, I'll work the means
To make thee capable.

Enter CORNWALL, REGAN *and Attendants.*

CORNWALL.
How now, my noble friend! since I came hither,
Which I can call but now, I have heard strange news.

REGAN.
If it be true, all vengeance comes too short
Which can pursue th'offender. How dost, my lord?

GLOUCESTER.
O madam, my old heart is crack'd, it's crack'd!

REGAN.
What, did my father's godson seek your life?
He whom my father nam'd? your Edgar?

GLOUCESTER.
O lady, lady, shame would have it hid!

REGAN.
Was he not companion with the riotous knights
That tend upon my father?

GLOUCESTER.
I know not, madam; 'tis too bad, too bad.

EDMUND.
Yes, madam, he was of that consort.

REGAN.
No marvel then though he were ill affected:
'Tis they have put him on the old man's death,
To have the expense and waste of his revenues.
I have this present evening from my sister
Been well inform'd of them; and with such cautions
That if they come to sojourn at my house,
I'll not be there.

CORNWALL.
Nor I, assure thee, Regan.
Edmund, I hear that you have shown your father
A childlike office.

EDMUND.
It was my duty, sir.

GLOUCESTER.
He did bewray his practice; and receiv'd
This hurt you see, striving to apprehend him.

CORNWALL.
Is he pursued?

GLOUCESTER.
Ay, my good lord.

CORNWALL.
If he be taken, he shall never more
Be fear'd of doing harm: make your own purpose,
How in my strength you please. For you, Edmund,
Whose virtue and obedience doth this instant
So much commend itself, you shall be ours:
Natures of such deep trust we shall much need;
You we first seize on.

EDMUND.
I shall serve you, sir, truly, however else.

GLOUCESTER.
For him I thank your grace.

CORNWALL.
You know not why we came to visit you?

REGAN.
Thus out of season, threading dark-ey'd night:
Occasions, noble Gloucester, of some poise,
Wherein we must have use of your advice.
Our father he hath writ, so hath our sister,
Of differences, which I best thought it fit
To answer from our home; the several messengers
From hence attend dispatch. Our good old friend,
Lay comforts to your bosom; and bestow
Your needful counsel to our business,
Which craves the instant use.

GLOUCESTER.
I serve you, madam:
Your graces are right welcome.

[*Exeunt. Flourish.*]

SCENE II. Before Gloucester's Castle.

Enter KENT AND OSWALD, *severally.*

OSWALD.
Good dawning to thee, friend: art of this house?

KENT.
Ay.

OSWALD.
Where may we set our horses?

KENT.
I' the mire.

OSWALD.
Prythee, if thou lov'st me, tell me.

KENT.
I love thee not.

OSWALD.
Why then, I care not for thee.

KENT.
If I had thee in Lipsbury pinfold, I would make thee care for me.

OSWALD.
Why dost thou use me thus? I know thee not.

KENT.
Fellow, I know thee.

OSWALD.
What dost thou know me for?

KENT.
A knave; a rascal; an eater of broken meats; a base, proud, shallow, beggarly, three-suited, hundred-pound, filthy, worsted-stocking knave; a lily-livered, action-taking, whoreson, glass-gazing, super-serviceable, finical rogue; one trunk-inheriting slave; one that wouldst be a bawd in way of good service, and art nothing but the composition of a knave, beggar, coward, pander, and the son and heir of a mongrel bitch: one whom I will beat into clamorous whining, if thou deniest the least syllable of thy addition.

OSWALD.
Why, what a monstrous fellow art thou, thus to rail on one that's neither known of thee nor knows thee?

KENT.
What a brazen-faced varlet art thou, to deny thou knowest me! Is it two days ago since

I tripped up thy heels and beat thee before the King? Draw, you rogue: for, though it be night, yet the moon shines; I'll make a sop o' the moonshine of you: draw, you whoreson cullionly barber-monger, draw!

[*Drawing his sword.*]

OSWALD.
Away! I have nothing to do with thee.

KENT.
Draw, you rascal: you come with letters against the King; and take vanity the puppet's part against the royalty of her father: draw, you rogue, or I'll so carbonado your shanks:—draw, you rascal; come your ways!

OSWALD.
Help, ho! murder! help!

KENT.
Strike, you slave; stand, rogue, stand; you neat slave, strike!

[*Beating him.*]

OSWALD.
Help, ho! murder! murder!

 Enter EDMUND, CORNWALL, REGAN, GLOUCESTER *and Servants.*

EDMUND.
How now! What's the matter? Part!

KENT.
With you, goodman boy, if you please: come, I'll flesh ye; come on, young master.

GLOUCESTER.
Weapons! arms! What's the matter here?

CORNWALL.
Keep peace, upon your lives, he dies that strikes again. What is the matter?

REGAN.
The messengers from our sister and the King.

CORNWALL.
What is your difference? Speak.

OSWALD.
I am scarce in breath, my lord.

KENT.
No marvel, you have so bestirr'd your valour. You cowardly rascal, nature disclaims in thee; a tailor made thee.

CORNWALL.
Thou art a strange fellow: a tailor make a man?

KENT.
Ay, a tailor, sir: a stonecutter or a painter could not have made him so ill, though he had been but two years at the trade.

CORNWALL.
Speak yet, how grew your quarrel?

OSWALD.
This ancient ruffian, sir, whose life I have spared at suit of his grey beard,—

KENT.
Thou whoreson zed! thou unnecessary letter! My lord, if you'll give me leave, I will tread this unbolted villain into mortar and daub the walls of a jakes with him. Spare my grey beard, you wagtail?

CORNWALL.
Peace, sirrah!
You beastly knave, know you no reverence?

KENT.
Yes, sir; but anger hath a privilege.

CORNWALL.
Why art thou angry?

KENT.
That such a slave as this should wear a sword,
Who wears no honesty. Such smiling rogues as these,
Like rats, oft bite the holy cords a-twain
Which are too intrince t'unloose; smooth every passion
That in the natures of their lords rebel;
Bring oil to fire, snow to their colder moods;
Renege, affirm, and turn their halcyon beaks
With every gale and vary of their masters,
Knowing naught, like dogs, but following.
A plague upon your epileptic visage!
Smile you my speeches, as I were a fool?
Goose, if I had you upon Sarum plain,
I'd drive ye cackling home to Camelot.

CORNWALL.
What, art thou mad, old fellow?

GLOUCESTER.
How fell you out? Say that.

KENT.
No contraries hold more antipathy
Than I and such a knave.

CORNWALL.
Why dost thou call him knave? What is his fault?

KENT.
His countenance likes me not.

CORNWALL.
No more perchance does mine, or his, or hers.

KENT.
Sir, 'tis my occupation to be plain:
I have seen better faces in my time
Than stands on any shoulder that I see
Before me at this instant.

CORNWALL.
This is some fellow
Who, having been prais'd for bluntness, doth affect
A saucy roughness, and constrains the garb
Quite from his nature: he cannot flatter, he,
An honest mind and plain, he must speak truth!
An they will take it, so; if not, he's plain.
These kind of knaves I know which in this plainness
Harbour more craft and more corrupter ends
Than twenty silly-ducking observants
That stretch their duties nicely.

KENT.
Sir, in good faith, in sincere verity,
Under th'allowance of your great aspect,
Whose influence, like the wreath of radiant fire
On flickering Phoebus' front,—

CORNWALL.
What mean'st by this?

KENT.
To go out of my dialect, which you discommend so much. I know, sir, I am no
flatterer: he that beguiled you in a plain accent was a plain knave; which, for my part,
I will not be, though I should win your displeasure to entreat me to't.

CORNWALL.
What was the offence you gave him?

OSWALD.
I never gave him any:
It pleas'd the King his master very late
To strike at me, upon his misconstruction;
When he, compact, and flattering his displeasure,
Tripp'd me behind; being down, insulted, rail'd
And put upon him such a deal of man,
That worthied him, got praises of the King
For him attempting who was self-subdu'd;
And, in the fleshment of this dread exploit,
Drew on me here again.

KENT.
None of these rogues and cowards
But Ajax is their fool.

CORNWALL.
Fetch forth the stocks!
You stubborn ancient knave, you reverent braggart,
We'll teach you.

KENT.
Sir, I am too old to learn:
Call not your stocks for me: I serve the King;
On whose employment I was sent to you:
You shall do small respect, show too bold malice
Against the grace and person of my master,
Stocking his messenger.

CORNWALL.
Fetch forth the stocks!
As I have life and honour, there shall he sit till noon.

REGAN.
Till noon! Till night, my lord; and all night too!

KENT.
Why, madam, if I were your father's dog,
You should not use me so.

REGAN.
Sir, being his knave, I will.

[*Stocks brought out.*]

CORNWALL.
This is a fellow of the selfsame colour
Our sister speaks of. Come, bring away the stocks!

GLOUCESTER.
Let me beseech your grace not to do so:
His fault is much, and the good King his master
Will check him for't: your purpos'd low correction
Is such as basest and contemned'st wretches
For pilferings and most common trespasses,
Are punish'd with. The King must take it ill
That he, so slightly valued in his messenger,
Should have him thus restrained.

CORNWALL.
I'll answer that.

REGAN.
My sister may receive it much more worse,
To have her gentleman abus'd, assaulted,
For following her affairs. Put in his legs.

[KENT *is put in the stocks.*]

CORNWALL.
Come, my good lord, away.

[*Exeunt all but* GLOUCESTER *and* KENT.]

GLOUCESTER.
I am sorry for thee, friend; 'tis the Duke's pleasure,
Whose disposition, all the world well knows,
Will not be rubb'd nor stopp'd; I'll entreat for thee.

KENT.
Pray do not, sir: I have watch'd, and travell'd hard;
Some time I shall sleep out, the rest I'll whistle.
A good man's fortune may grow out at heels:
Give you good morrow!

GLOUCESTER.
The Duke's to blame in this: 'twill be ill taken.

[*Exit.*]

KENT.
Good King, that must approve the common saw,
Thou out of heaven's benediction com'st

To the warm sun.
Approach, thou beacon to this under globe,
That by thy comfortable beams I may
Peruse this letter. Nothing almost sees miracles
But misery. I know 'tis from Cordelia,
Who hath most fortunately been inform'd
Of my obscured course. And shall find time
From this enormous state, seeking to give
Losses their remedies. All weary and o'erwatch'd,
Take vantage, heavy eyes, not to behold
This shameful lodging.
Fortune, good night: smile once more, turn thy wheel!

[*He sleeps.*]

SCENE III. The open Country.

Enter EDGAR.

EDGAR.
I heard myself proclaim'd,
And by the happy hollow of a tree
Escap'd the hunt. No port is free, no place
That guard and most unusual vigilance
Does not attend my taking. While I may scape
I will preserve myself: and am bethought
To take the basest and most poorest shape
That ever penury in contempt of man,
Brought near to beast: my face I'll grime with filth,
Blanket my loins; elf all my hair in knots,
And with presented nakedness outface
The winds and persecutions of the sky.
The country gives me proof and precedent
Of Bedlam beggars, who, with roaring voices,
Strike in their numb'd and mortified bare arms
Pins, wooden pricks, nails, sprigs of rosemary;
And with this horrible object, from low farms,
Poor pelting villages, sheep-cotes, and mills,
Sometime with lunatic bans, sometime with prayers,
Enforce their charity. Poor Turlygod! poor Tom,
That's something yet: Edgar I nothing am.

[*Exit.*]

SCENE IV. Before Gloucester's Castle; Kent in the stocks.

Enter LEAR, FOOL *and* GENTLEMAN.

LEAR.
'Tis strange that they should so depart from home,
And not send back my messenger.

GENTLEMAN.
As I learn'd,
The night before there was no purpose in them
Of this remove.

KENT.
Hail to thee, noble master!

LEAR.
Ha! Mak'st thou this shame thy pastime?

KENT.
No, my lord.

FOOL.
Ha, ha! he wears cruel garters. Horses are tied by the heads; dogs and bears by the neck, monkeys by the loins, and men by the legs: when a man is overlusty at legs, then he wears wooden nether-stocks.

LEAR.
What's he that hath so much thy place mistook
To set thee here?

KENT.
It is both he and she,
Your son and daughter.

LEAR.
No.

KENT.
Yes.

LEAR.
No, I say.

KENT.
I say, yea.

LEAR.
No, no; they would not.

KENT.
Yes, they have.

LEAR.
By Jupiter, I swear no.

KENT.
By Juno, I swear ay.

LEAR.
They durst not do't.
They could not, would not do't; 'tis worse than murder,
To do upon respect such violent outrage:
Resolve me, with all modest haste, which way
Thou mightst deserve or they impose this usage,
Coming from us.

KENT.
My lord, when at their home
I did commend your highness' letters to them,
Ere I was risen from the place that show'd
My duty kneeling, came there a reeking post,
Stew'd in his haste, half breathless, panting forth
From Goneril his mistress salutations;
Deliver'd letters, spite of intermission,
Which presently they read; on those contents,
They summon'd up their meiny, straight took horse;
Commanded me to follow and attend
The leisure of their answer; gave me cold looks:
And meeting here the other messenger,
Whose welcome I perceiv'd had poison'd mine,
Being the very fellow which of late
Display'd so saucily against your highness,
Having more man than wit about me, drew;
He rais'd the house with loud and coward cries.
Your son and daughter found this trespass worth
The shame which here it suffers.

FOOL.
Winter's not gone yet, if the wild geese fly that way.
  Fathers that wear rags
    Do make their children blind,
  But fathers that bear bags
    Shall see their children kind.

Fortune, that arrant whore,
  Ne'er turns the key to th' poor.
But for all this, thou shalt have as many dolours for thy daughters as thou canst tell in
a year.

LEAR.
O, how this mother swells up toward my heart!
Hysterica passio, down, thou climbing sorrow,
Thy element's below! Where is this daughter?

KENT.
With the earl, sir, here within.

LEAR.
Follow me not; stay here.

[*Exit.*]

GENTLEMAN.
Made you no more offence but what you speak of?

KENT.
None.
How chance the King comes with so small a number?

FOOL.
An thou hadst been set i' the stocks for that question, thou hadst well deserved it.

KENT.
Why, fool?

FOOL.
We'll set thee to school to an ant, to teach thee there's no labouring i'the winter. All
that follow their noses are led by their eyes but blind men; and there's not a nose
among twenty but can smell him that's stinking. Let go thy hold when a great wheel
runs down a hill, lest it break thy neck with following it; but the great one that goes
upward, let him draw thee after. When a wise man gives thee better counsel, give me
mine again: I would have none but knaves follow it, since a fool gives it.
  That sir which serves and seeks for gain,
    And follows but for form,
  Will pack when it begins to rain,
    And leave thee in the storm.
  But I will tarry; the fool will stay,
    And let the wise man fly:
  The knave turns fool that runs away;
    The fool no knave perdy.

KENT.
Where learn'd you this, fool?

FOOL.
Not i' the stocks, fool.

Enter LEAR *and* GLOUCESTER.

LEAR.
Deny to speak with me? They are sick? they are weary?
They have travell'd all the night? Mere fetches;
The images of revolt and flying off.
Fetch me a better answer.

GLOUCESTER.
My dear lord,
You know the fiery quality of the Duke;
How unremovable and fix'd he is
In his own course.

LEAR.
Vengeance! plague! death! confusion!
Fiery? What quality? Why, Gloucester, Gloucester,
I'd speak with the Duke of Cornwall and his wife.

GLOUCESTER.
Well, my good lord, I have inform'd them so.

LEAR.
Inform'd them! Dost thou understand me, man?

GLOUCESTER.
Ay, my good lord.

LEAR.
The King would speak with Cornwall; the dear father
Would with his daughter speak, commands, tends, service,
Are they inform'd of this? My breath and blood!
Fiery? The fiery Duke, tell the hot Duke that—
No, but not yet: maybe he is not well:
Infirmity doth still neglect all office
Whereto our health is bound: we are not ourselves
When nature, being oppress'd, commands the mind
To suffer with the body: I'll forbear;
And am fallen out with my more headier will,
To take the indispos'd and sickly fit
For the sound man. [*Looking on Kent.*]

Death on my state! Wherefore
Should he sit here? This act persuades me
That this remotion of the Duke and her
Is practice only. Give me my servant forth.
Go tell the Duke and's wife I'd speak with them,
Now, presently: bid them come forth and hear me,
Or at their chamber door I'll beat the drum
Till it cry sleep to death.

GLOUCESTER.
I would have all well betwixt you.

[*Exit.*]

LEAR.
O me, my heart, my rising heart! But down!

FOOL.
Cry to it, nuncle, as the cockney did to the eels when she put 'em i' the paste alive;
she knapped 'em o' the coxcombs with a stick and cried 'Down, wantons, down!'
'Twas her brother that, in pure kindness to his horse buttered his hay.

Enter CORNWALL, REGAN, GLOUCESTER *and Servants.*

LEAR.
Good morrow to you both.

CORNWALL.
Hail to your grace!

[KENT *here set at liberty.*]

REGAN.
I am glad to see your highness.

LEAR.
Regan, I think you are; I know what reason
I have to think so: if thou shouldst not be glad,
I would divorce me from thy mother's tomb,
Sepulchring an adultress. [*To Kent*] O, are you free?
Some other time for that.—Beloved Regan,
Thy sister's naught: O Regan, she hath tied
Sharp-tooth'd unkindness, like a vulture, here.

[*Points to his heart.*]

I can scarce speak to thee; thou'lt not believe
With how deprav'd a quality—O Regan!

REGAN.
I pray you, sir, take patience. I have hope
You less know how to value her desert
Than she to scant her duty.

LEAR.
Say, how is that?

REGAN.
I cannot think my sister in the least
Would fail her obligation. If, sir, perchance
She have restrain'd the riots of your followers,
'Tis on such ground, and to such wholesome end,
As clears her from all blame.

LEAR.
My curses on her.

REGAN.
O, sir, you are old;
Nature in you stands on the very verge
Of her confine: you should be rul'd and led
By some discretion, that discerns your state
Better than you yourself. Therefore I pray you,
That to our sister you do make return;
Say you have wrong'd her, sir.

LEAR.
Ask her forgiveness?
Do you but mark how this becomes the house?
'Dear daughter, I confess that I am old;
[*Kneeling.*]
Age is unnecessary: on my knees I beg
That you'll vouchsafe me raiment, bed, and food.'

REGAN.
Good sir, no more! These are unsightly tricks:
Return you to my sister.

LEAR.
[*Rising.*] Never, Regan:
She hath abated me of half my train;
Look'd black upon me; struck me with her tongue,
Most serpent-like, upon the very heart.
All the stor'd vengeances of heaven fall

On her ingrateful top! Strike her young bones,
You taking airs, with lameness!

CORNWALL.
Fie, sir, fie!

LEAR.
You nimble lightnings, dart your blinding flames
Into her scornful eyes! Infect her beauty,
You fen-suck'd fogs, drawn by the powerful sun,
To fall and blast her pride!

REGAN.
O the blest gods!
So will you wish on me when the rash mood is on.

LEAR.
No, Regan, thou shalt never have my curse.
Thy tender-hefted nature shall not give
Thee o'er to harshness. Her eyes are fierce; but thine
Do comfort, and not burn. 'Tis not in thee
To grudge my pleasures, to cut off my train,
To bandy hasty words, to scant my sizes,
And, in conclusion, to oppose the bolt
Against my coming in. Thou better know'st
The offices of nature, bond of childhood,
Effects of courtesy, dues of gratitude;
Thy half o' the kingdom hast thou not forgot,
Wherein I thee endow'd.

REGAN.
Good sir, to the purpose.

LEAR.
Who put my man i' the stocks?

[*Tucket within.*]

CORNWALL.
What trumpet's that?

REGAN.
I know't, my sister's: this approves her letter,
That she would soon be here.

   Enter OSWALD.

Is your lady come?

LEAR.
This is a slave, whose easy borrowed pride
Dwells in the fickle grace of her he follows.
Out, varlet, from my sight!

CORNWALL.
What means your grace?

LEAR.
Who stock'd my servant? Regan, I have good hope
Thou didst not know on't. Who comes here? O heavens!

    Enter GONERIL.

If you do love old men, if your sweet sway
Allow obedience, if yourselves are old,
Make it your cause; send down, and take my part!
[*To Goneril.*] Art not asham'd to look upon this beard?
O Regan, wilt thou take her by the hand?

GONERIL.
Why not by the hand, sir? How have I offended?
All's not offence that indiscretion finds
And dotage terms so.

LEAR.
O sides, you are too tough!
Will you yet hold? How came my man i' the stocks?

CORNWALL.
I set him there, sir: but his own disorders
Deserv'd much less advancement.

LEAR.
You? Did you?

REGAN.
I pray you, father, being weak, seem so.
If, till the expiration of your month,
You will return and sojourn with my sister,
Dismissing half your train, come then to me:
I am now from home, and out of that provision
Which shall be needful for your entertainment.

LEAR.
Return to her, and fifty men dismiss'd?
No, rather I abjure all roofs, and choose

To wage against the enmity o' the air;
To be a comrade with the wolf and owl,
Necessity's sharp pinch! Return with her?
Why, the hot-blooded France, that dowerless took
Our youngest born, I could as well be brought
To knee his throne, and, squire-like, pension beg
To keep base life afoot. Return with her?
Persuade me rather to be slave and sumpter
To this detested groom.

[*Pointing to Oswald.*]

GONERIL.
At your choice, sir.

LEAR.
I prythee, daughter, do not make me mad:
I will not trouble thee, my child; farewell:
We'll no more meet, no more see one another.
But yet thou art my flesh, my blood, my daughter;
Or rather a disease that's in my flesh,
Which I must needs call mine. Thou art a boil,
A plague sore, or embossed carbuncle
In my corrupted blood. But I'll not chide thee;
Let shame come when it will, I do not call it:
I do not bid the thunder-bearer shoot,
Nor tell tales of thee to high-judging Jove:
Mend when thou canst; be better at thy leisure:
I can be patient; I can stay with Regan,
I and my hundred knights.

REGAN.
Not altogether so,
I look'd not for you yet, nor am provided
For your fit welcome. Give ear, sir, to my sister;
For those that mingle reason with your passion
Must be content to think you old, and so—
But she knows what she does.

LEAR.
Is this well spoken?

REGAN.
I dare avouch it, sir: what, fifty followers?
Is it not well? What should you need of more?

Yea, or so many, sith that both charge and danger
Speak 'gainst so great a number? How in one house
Should many people, under two commands,
Hold amity? 'Tis hard; almost impossible.

GONERIL.
Why might not you, my lord, receive attendance
From those that she calls servants, or from mine?

REGAN.
Why not, my lord? If then they chanc'd to slack ye,
We could control them. If you will come to me,—
For now I spy a danger,—I entreat you
To bring but five-and-twenty: to no more
Will I give place or notice.

LEAR.
I gave you all,—

REGAN.
And in good time you gave it.

LEAR.
Made you my guardians, my depositaries;
But kept a reservation to be followed
With such a number. What, must I come to you
With five-and-twenty, Regan, said you so?

REGAN.
And speak't again my lord; no more with me.

LEAR.
Those wicked creatures yet do look well-favour'd
When others are more wicked; not being the worst
Stands in some rank of praise.
[*To Goneril.*] I'll go with thee:
Thy fifty yet doth double five-and-twenty,
And thou art twice her love.

GONERIL.
Hear me, my lord:
What need you five-and-twenty? Ten? Or five?
To follow in a house where twice so many
Have a command to tend you?

REGAN.
What need one?

LEAR.

O, reason not the need: our basest beggars
Are in the poorest thing superfluous:
Allow not nature more than nature needs,
Man's life is cheap as beast's. Thou art a lady;
If only to go warm were gorgeous,
Why, nature needs not what thou gorgeous wear'st
Which scarcely keeps thee warm. But, for true need,—
You heavens, give me that patience, patience I need!
You see me here, you gods, a poor old man,
As full of grief as age; wretched in both!
If it be you that stirs these daughters' hearts
Against their father, fool me not so much
To bear it tamely; touch me with noble anger,
And let not women's weapons, water-drops,
Stain my man's cheeks! No, you unnatural hags,
I will have such revenges on you both
That all the world shall,—I will do such things,—
What they are yet, I know not; but they shall be
The terrors of the earth. You think I'll weep;
No, I'll not weep:— [*Storm and tempest.*]
I have full cause of weeping; but this heart
Shall break into a hundred thousand flaws
Or ere I'll weep.—O fool, I shall go mad!

[*Exeunt* LEAR, GLOUCESTER, KENT *and* FOOL.]

CORNWALL.

Let us withdraw; 'twill be a storm.

REGAN.

This house is little: the old man and his people
Cannot be well bestow'd.

GONERIL.

'Tis his own blame; hath put himself from rest
And must needs taste his folly.

REGAN.

For his particular, I'll receive him gladly,
But not one follower.

GONERIL.

So am I purpos'd.
Where is my lord of Gloucester?

Enter GLOUCESTER.

CORNWALL.
Followed the old man forth, he is return'd.

GLOUCESTER.
The King is in high rage.

CORNWALL.
Whither is he going?

GLOUCESTER.
He calls to horse; but will I know not whither.

CORNWALL.
'Tis best to give him way; he leads himself.

GONERIL.
My lord, entreat him by no means to stay.

GLOUCESTER.
Alack, the night comes on, and the high winds
Do sorely ruffle; for many miles about
There's scarce a bush.

REGAN.
O, sir, to wilful men
The injuries that they themselves procure
Must be their schoolmasters. Shut up your doors.
He is attended with a desperate train,
And what they may incense him to, being apt
To have his ear abus'd, wisdom bids fear.

CORNWALL.
Shut up your doors, my lord; 'tis a wild night.
My Regan counsels well: come out o' the storm.

[*Exeunt.*]

ACT III

SCENE I. A Heath.

A storm with thunder and lightning. Enter KENT *and a* GENTLEMAN, *severally.*

KENT.
Who's there, besides foul weather?

GENTLEMAN.
One minded like the weather, most unquietly.

KENT.
I know you. Where's the King?

GENTLEMAN.
Contending with the fretful elements;
Bids the wind blow the earth into the sea,
Or swell the curled waters 'bove the main,
That things might change or cease; tears his white hair,
Which the impetuous blasts with eyeless rage,
Catch in their fury and make nothing of;
Strives in his little world of man to outscorn
The to-and-fro-conflicting wind and rain.
This night, wherein the cub-drawn bear would couch,
The lion and the belly-pinched wolf
Keep their fur dry, unbonneted he runs,
And bids what will take all.

KENT.
But who is with him?

GENTLEMAN.
None but the fool, who labours to out-jest
His heart-struck injuries.

KENT.
Sir, I do know you;
And dare, upon the warrant of my note
Commend a dear thing to you. There is division,
Although as yet the face of it be cover'd
With mutual cunning, 'twixt Albany and Cornwall;
Who have, as who have not, that their great stars
Throne'd and set high; servants, who seem no less,
Which are to France the spies and speculations
Intelligent of our state. What hath been seen,
Either in snuffs and packings of the Dukes;
Or the hard rein which both of them have borne
Against the old kind King; or something deeper,
Whereof, perchance, these are but furnishings;—
But, true it is, from France there comes a power

Into this scatter'd kingdom; who already,
Wise in our negligence, have secret feet
In some of our best ports, and are at point
To show their open banner.—Now to you:
If on my credit you dare build so far
To make your speed to Dover, you shall find
Some that will thank you making just report
Of how unnatural and bemadding sorrow
The King hath cause to plain.
I am a gentleman of blood and breeding;
And from some knowledge and assurance
Offer this office to you.

GENTLEMAN.
I will talk further with you.

KENT.
No, do not.
For confirmation that I am much more
Than my out-wall, open this purse, and take
What it contains. If you shall see Cordelia,
As fear not but you shall, show her this ring;
And she will tell you who your fellow is
That yet you do not know. Fie on this storm!
I will go seek the King.

GENTLEMAN.
Give me your hand: have you no more to say?

KENT.
Few words, but, to effect, more than all yet:
That, when we have found the King, in which your pain
That way, I'll this; he that first lights on him
Holla the other.

[*Exeunt.*]

SCENE II. Another part of the heath.

Storm continues. Enter LEAR *and* FOOL.

LEAR.
Blow, winds, and crack your cheeks! Rage! blow!
You cataracts and hurricanoes, spout
Till you have drench'd our steeples, drown'd the cocks!
You sulphurous and thought-executing fires,

Vaunt-couriers to oak-cleaving thunderbolts,
Singe my white head! And thou, all-shaking thunder,
Strike flat the thick rotundity o' the world!
Crack nature's moulds, all germens spill at once,
That make ingrateful man!

FOOL.
O nuncle, court holy-water in a dry house is better than this rain-water out o' door.
Good nuncle, in; and ask thy daughters blessing: here's a night pities neither wise men
nor fools.

LEAR.
Rumble thy bellyful! Spit, fire! spout, rain!
Nor rain, wind, thunder, fire are my daughters;
I tax not you, you elements, with unkindness.
I never gave you kingdom, call'd you children;
You owe me no subscription: then let fall
Your horrible pleasure. Here I stand your slave,
A poor, infirm, weak, and despis'd old man:
But yet I call you servile ministers,
That will with two pernicious daughters join
Your high-engender'd battles 'gainst a head
So old and white as this! O! O! 'tis foul!

FOOL.
He that has a house to put's head in has a good head-piece.
    The codpiece that will house
        Before the head has any,
    The head and he shall louse:
        So beggars marry many.
    The man that makes his toe
        What he his heart should make
    Shall of a corn cry woe,
        And turn his sleep to wake.
For there was never yet fair woman but she made mouths in a glass.

LEAR.
No, I will be the pattern of all patience;
I will say nothing.

    Enter KENT.

KENT.
Who's there?

FOOL.
Marry, here's grace and a codpiece; that's a wise man and a fool.

KENT.
Alas, sir, are you here? Things that love night
Love not such nights as these; the wrathful skies
Gallow the very wanderers of the dark,
And make them keep their caves. Since I was man,
Such sheets of fire, such bursts of horrid thunder,
Such groans of roaring wind and rain I never
Remember to have heard. Man's nature cannot carry
Th'affliction, nor the fear.

LEAR.
Let the great gods,
That keep this dreadful pudder o'er our heads,
Find out their enemies now. Tremble, thou wretch,
That hast within thee undivulged crimes
Unwhipp'd of justice. Hide thee, thou bloody hand;
Thou perjur'd, and thou simular of virtue
That art incestuous. Caitiff, to pieces shake
That under covert and convenient seeming
Hast practis'd on man's life: close pent-up guilts,
Rive your concealing continents, and cry
These dreadful summoners grace. I am a man
More sinn'd against than sinning.

KENT.
Alack, bareheaded!
Gracious my lord, hard by here is a hovel;
Some friendship will it lend you 'gainst the tempest:
Repose you there, whilst I to this hard house,—
More harder than the stones whereof 'tis rais'd;
Which even but now, demanding after you,
Denied me to come in,—return, and force
Their scanted courtesy.

LEAR.
My wits begin to turn.
Come on, my boy. How dost, my boy? Art cold?
I am cold myself. Where is this straw, my fellow?
The art of our necessities is strange,
That can make vile things precious. Come, your hovel.

Poor fool and knave, I have one part in my heart
That's sorry yet for thee.

FOOL.
[*Singing.*]
  He that has and a little tiny wit,
    With heigh-ho, the wind and the rain,
  Must make content with his fortunes fit,
    Though the rain it raineth every day.

LEAR.
True, boy. Come, bring us to this hovel.

[*Exeunt* LEAR *and* KENT.]

FOOL.
This is a brave night to cool a courtezan. I'll speak a prophecy ere I go:
  When priests are more in word than matter;
  When brewers mar their malt with water;
  When nobles are their tailors' tutors;
  No heretics burn'd, but wenches' suitors;
  When every case in law is right;
  No squire in debt, nor no poor knight;
  When slanders do not live in tongues;
  Nor cut-purses come not to throngs;
  When usurers tell their gold i' the field;
  And bawds and whores do churches build,
  Then shall the realm of Albion
  Come to great confusion:
  Then comes the time, who lives to see't,
  That going shall be us'd with feet.
This prophecy Merlin shall make; for I live before his time.

[*Exit.*]

SCENE III. A Room in Gloucester's Castle.

Enter GLOUCESTER *and* EDMUND.

GLOUCESTER.
Alack, alack, Edmund, I like not this unnatural dealing. When I desired their leave that I might pity him, they took from me the use of mine own house; charged me on pain of perpetual displeasure, neither to speak of him, entreat for him, or any way sustain him.

EDMUND.
Most savage and unnatural!

GLOUCESTER.
Go to; say you nothing. There is division between the Dukes, and a worse matter than that: I have received a letter this night;—'tis dangerous to be spoken;—I have locked the letter in my closet: these injuries the King now bears will be revenged home; there's part of a power already footed: we must incline to the King. I will look him, and privily relieve him: go you and maintain talk with the Duke, that my charity be not of him perceived: if he ask for me, I am ill, and gone to bed. If I die for it, as no less is threatened me, the King my old master must be relieved. There is some strange thing toward, Edmund; pray you be careful.

[*Exit.*]

EDMUND.
This courtesy, forbid thee, shall the Duke
Instantly know; and of that letter too.
This seems a fair deserving, and must draw me
That which my father loses, no less than all:
The younger rises when the old doth fall.

[*Exit.*]

SCENE IV. A part of the Heath with a Hovel.

Storm continues. Enter LEAR, KENT *and* FOOL.

KENT.
Here is the place, my lord; good my lord, enter:
The tyranny of the open night's too rough
For nature to endure.

LEAR.
Let me alone.

KENT.
Good my lord, enter here.

LEAR.
Wilt break my heart?

KENT.
I had rather break mine own. Good my lord, enter.

LEAR.
Thou think'st 'tis much that this contentious storm
Invades us to the skin: so 'tis to thee,

But where the greater malady is fix'd,
The lesser is scarce felt. Thou'dst shun a bear;
But if thy flight lay toward the raging sea,
Thou'dst meet the bear i' the mouth. When the mind's free,
The body's delicate: the tempest in my mind
Doth from my senses take all feeling else
Save what beats there. Filial ingratitude!
Is it not as this mouth should tear this hand
For lifting food to't? But I will punish home;
No, I will weep no more. In such a night
To shut me out! Pour on; I will endure:
In such a night as this! O Regan, Goneril!
Your old kind father, whose frank heart gave all,
O, that way madness lies; let me shun that;
No more of that.

KENT.
Good my lord, enter here.

LEAR.
Prythee go in thyself; seek thine own ease:
This tempest will not give me leave to ponder
On things would hurt me more. But I'll go in.
[*To the Fool.*] In, boy; go first. You houseless poverty,
Nay, get thee in. I'll pray, and then I'll sleep.

[FOOL *goes in.*]

Poor naked wretches, wheresoe'er you are,
That bide the pelting of this pitiless storm,
How shall your houseless heads and unfed sides,
Your loop'd and window'd raggedness, defend you
From seasons such as these? O, I have ta'en
Too little care of this! Take physic, pomp;
Expose thyself to feel what wretches feel,
That thou mayst shake the superflux to them
And show the heavens more just.

EDGAR.
[*Within.*] Fathom and half, fathom and half! Poor Tom!

[*The* FOOL *runs out from the hovel.*]

FOOL.
Come not in here, nuncle, here's a spirit.
Help me, help me!

KENT.
Give me thy hand. Who's there?

FOOL.
A spirit, a spirit: he says his name's poor Tom.

KENT.
What art thou that dost grumble there i' the straw?
Come forth.

Enter EDGAR, *disguised as a madman.*

EDGAR.
Away! the foul fiend follows me! Through the sharp hawthorn blows the cold wind.
Humh! go to thy cold bed, and warm thee.

LEAR.
Didst thou give all to thy two daughters?
And art thou come to this?

EDGAR.
Who gives anything to poor Tom? Whom the foul fiend hath led through fire and
through flame, through ford and whirlpool, o'er bog and quagmire; that hath laid
knives under his pillow and halters in his pew, set ratsbane by his porridge; made him
proud of heart, to ride on a bay trotting horse over four-inched bridges, to course his
own shadow for a traitor. Bless thy five wits! Tom's a-cold. O, do, de, do, de, do, de.
Bless thee from whirlwinds, star-blasting, and taking! Do poor Tom some charity,
whom the foul fiend vexes. There could I have him now, and there,—and there again,
and there.

[*Storm continues.*]

LEAR.
What, have his daughters brought him to this pass?
Couldst thou save nothing? Didst thou give 'em all?

FOOL.
Nay, he reserv'd a blanket, else we had been all shamed.

LEAR.
Now all the plagues that in the pendulous air
Hang fated o'er men's faults light on thy daughters!

KENT.
He hath no daughters, sir.

LEAR.
Death, traitor! nothing could have subdu'd nature
To such a lowness but his unkind daughters.

Is it the fashion that discarded fathers
Should have thus little mercy on their flesh?
Judicious punishment! 'twas this flesh begot
Those pelican daughters.

EDGAR.
  Pillicock sat on Pillicock hill,
    Alow, alow, loo loo!

FOOL.
This cold night will turn us all to fools and madmen.

EDGAR.
Take heed o' th' foul fiend: obey thy parents; keep thy word justly; swear not; commit
not with man's sworn spouse; set not thy sweet-heart on proud array. Tom's a-cold.

LEAR.
What hast thou been?

EDGAR.
A serving-man, proud in heart and mind; that curled my hair; wore gloves in my cap;
served the lust of my mistress' heart, and did the act of darkness with her; swore as
many oaths as I spake words, and broke them in the sweet face of heaven. One that
slept in the contriving of lust, and waked to do it. Wine loved I deeply, dice dearly;
and in woman out-paramour'd the Turk. False of heart, light of ear, bloody of hand;
hog in sloth, fox in stealth, wolf in greediness, dog in madness, lion in prey. Let not
the creaking of shoes nor the rustling of silks betray thy poor heart to woman. Keep
thy foot out of brothels, thy hand out of plackets, thy pen from lender's book, and
defy the foul fiend. Still through the hawthorn blows the cold wind: says suum, mun,
nonny. Dolphin my boy, boy, sessa! let him trot by.

[*Storm still continues.*]

LEAR.
Why, thou wert better in thy grave than to answer with thy uncovered body this
extremity of the skies. Is man no more than this? Consider him well. Thou owest the
worm no silk, the beast no hide, the sheep no wool, the cat no perfume. Ha! here's
three on's are sophisticated! Thou art the thing itself: unaccommodated man is no
more but such a poor, bare, forked animal as thou art. Off, off, you lendings! Come,
unbutton here.

[*Tears off his clothes.*]

FOOL.
Prythee, nuncle, be contented; 'tis a naughty night to swim in. Now a little fire in a
wild field were like an old lecher's heart, a small spark, all the rest on's body cold.
Look, here comes a walking fire.

EDGAR.
This is the foul fiend Flibbertigibbet: he begins at curfew, and walks till the first cock; he gives the web and the pin, squints the eye, and makes the harelip; mildews the white wheat, and hurts the poor creature of earth.

Swithold footed thrice the old;
He met the nightmare, and her nine-fold;
Bid her alight and her troth plight,
And aroint thee, witch, aroint thee!

KENT.
How fares your grace?

Enter GLOUCESTER *with a torch.*

LEAR.
What's he?

KENT.
Who's there? What is't you seek?

GLOUCESTER.
What are you there? Your names?

EDGAR.
Poor Tom; that eats the swimming frog, the toad, the todpole, the wall-newt and the water; that in the fury of his heart, when the foul fiend rages, eats cow-dung for sallets; swallows the old rat and the ditch-dog; drinks the green mantle of the standing pool; who is whipped from tithing to tithing, and stocked, punished, and imprisoned; who hath had three suits to his back, six shirts to his body,

Horse to ride, and weapon to wear.
But mice and rats and such small deer,
Have been Tom's food for seven long year.
Beware my follower. Peace, Smulkin; peace, thou fiend!

GLOUCESTER.
What, hath your grace no better company?

EDGAR.
The prince of darkness is a gentleman:
Modo he's call'd, and Mahu.

GLOUCESTER.
Our flesh and blood, my lord, is grown so vile
That it doth hate what gets it.

EDGAR.
Poor Tom's a-cold.

GLOUCESTER.
Go in with me: my duty cannot suffer
T'obey in all your daughters' hard commands;
Though their injunction be to bar my doors,
And let this tyrannous night take hold upon you,
Yet have I ventur'd to come seek you out,
And bring you where both fire and food is ready.

LEAR.
First let me talk with this philosopher.
What is the cause of thunder?

KENT.
Good my lord, take his offer; go into the house.

LEAR.
I'll talk a word with this same learned Theban.
What is your study?

EDGAR.
How to prevent the fiend and to kill vermin.

LEAR.
Let me ask you one word in private.

KENT.
Importune him once more to go, my lord;
His wits begin t'unsettle.

GLOUCESTER.
Canst thou blame him?
His daughters seek his death. Ah, that good Kent!
He said it would be thus, poor banish'd man!
Thou sayest the King grows mad; I'll tell thee, friend,
I am almost mad myself. I had a son,
Now outlaw'd from my blood; he sought my life
But lately, very late: I lov'd him, friend,
No father his son dearer: true to tell thee,

[*Storm continues.*]

The grief hath craz'd my wits. What a night's this!
I do beseech your grace.

LEAR.
O, cry you mercy, sir.
Noble philosopher, your company.

EDGAR.
Tom's a-cold.

GLOUCESTER.
In, fellow, there, into the hovel; keep thee warm.

LEAR.
Come, let's in all.

KENT.
This way, my lord.

LEAR.
With him;
I will keep still with my philosopher.

KENT.
Good my lord, soothe him; let him take the fellow.

GLOUCESTER.
Take him you on.

KENT.
Sirrah, come on; go along with us.

LEAR.
Come, good Athenian.

GLOUCESTER.
No words, no words, hush.

EDGAR.
　　Child Rowland to the dark tower came,
　　His word was still—Fie, foh, and fum,
　　I smell the blood of a British man.

[*Exeunt.*]

SCENE V. A Room in Gloucester's Castle.

Enter CORNWALL *and* EDMUND.

CORNWALL.
I will have my revenge ere I depart his house.

EDMUND.
How, my lord, I may be censured, that nature thus gives way to loyalty, something fears me to think of.

CORNWALL.
I now perceive it was not altogether your brother's evil disposition made him seek his death; but a provoking merit, set a-work by a reproveable badness in himself.

EDMUND.
How malicious is my fortune, that I must repent to be just! This is the letter he spoke of, which approves him an intelligent party to the advantages of France. O heavens! that this treason were not; or not I the detector!

CORNWALL.
Go with me to the Duchess.

EDMUND.
If the matter of this paper be certain, you have mighty business in hand.

CORNWALL.
True or false, it hath made thee Earl of Gloucester. Seek out where thy father is, that he may be ready for our apprehension.

EDMUND.
[*Aside.*] If I find him comforting the King, it will stuff his suspicion more fully. I will persever in my course of loyalty, though the conflict be sore between that and my blood.

CORNWALL.
I will lay trust upon thee; and thou shalt find a dearer father in my love.

[*Exeunt.*]

SCENE VI. A Chamber in a Farmhouse adjoining the Castle.

Enter GLOUCESTER, LEAR, KENT, FOOL *and* EDGAR.

GLOUCESTER.
Here is better than the open air; take it thankfully. I will piece out the comfort with what addition I can: I will not be long from you.

KENT.
All the power of his wits have given way to his impatience:— the gods reward your kindness!

[*Exit* GLOUCESTER.]

EDGAR.
Fraterretto calls me; and tells me Nero is an angler in the lake of darkness. Pray, innocent, and beware the foul fiend.

FOOL.
Prythee, nuncle, tell me whether a madman be a gentleman or a yeoman.

LEAR.
A king, a king!

FOOL.
No, he's a yeoman that has a gentleman to his son; for he's a mad yeoman that sees his son a gentleman before him.

LEAR.
To have a thousand with red burning spits
Come hissing in upon 'em.

EDGAR.
The foul fiend bites my back.

FOOL.
He's mad that trusts in the tameness of a wolf, a horse's health, a boy's love, or a whore's oath.

LEAR.
It shall be done; I will arraign them straight.
[*To Edgar.*] Come, sit thou here, most learned justicer;
[*To the Fool.*] Thou, sapient sir, sit here. Now, you she-foxes!—

EDGAR.
Look, where he stands and glares! Want'st thou eyes at trial, madam?
  Come o'er the bourn, Bessy, to me.

FOOL.
  Her boat hath a leak,
  And she must not speak
  Why she dares not come over to thee.

EDGAR.
The foul fiend haunts poor Tom in the voice of a nightingale. Hoppedance cries in Tom's belly for two white herring. Croak not, black angel; I have no food for thee.

KENT.
How do you, sir? Stand you not so amaz'd;
Will you lie down and rest upon the cushions?

LEAR.
I'll see their trial first. Bring in their evidence.
[*To Edgar.*] Thou, robed man of justice, take thy place.
[*To the Fool.*] And thou, his yokefellow of equity,
Bench by his side. [*To Kent.*] You are o' the commission,
Sit you too.

EDGAR.
Let us deal justly.
  Sleepest or wakest thou, jolly shepherd?
    Thy sheep be in the corn;
  And for one blast of thy minikin mouth
    Thy sheep shall take no harm.
Purr! the cat is grey.

LEAR.
Arraign her first; 'tis Goneril. I here take my oath before this honourable assembly,
she kicked the poor King her father.

FOOL.
Come hither, mistress. Is your name Goneril?

LEAR.
She cannot deny it.

FOOL.
Cry you mercy, I took you for a joint-stool.

LEAR.
And here's another, whose warp'd looks proclaim
What store her heart is made on. Stop her there!
Arms, arms! sword! fire! Corruption in the place!
False justicer, why hast thou let her 'scape?

EDGAR.
Bless thy five wits!

KENT.
O pity! Sir, where is the patience now
That you so oft have boasted to retain?

EDGAR.
[*Aside.*] My tears begin to take his part so much
They mar my counterfeiting.

LEAR.
The little dogs and all,
Trey, Blanch, and Sweetheart, see, they bark at me.

EDGAR.
Tom will throw his head at them. Avaunt, you curs!
  Be thy mouth or black or white,
  Tooth that poisons if it bite;
  Mastiff, greyhound, mongrel grim,

Hound or spaniel, brach or him,
Or bobtail tike or trundle-tail,
Tom will make them weep and wail;
For, with throwing thus my head,
Dogs leap the hatch, and all are fled.

Do, de, de, de. Sessa! Come, march to wakes and fairs and market towns. Poor Tom, thy horn is dry.

LEAR.
Then let them anatomize Regan; see what breeds about her heart. Is there any cause in nature that makes these hard hearts? [*To Edgar.*] You, sir, I entertain you for one of my hundred; only I do not like the fashion of your garments. You'll say they are Persian; but let them be changed.

KENT.
Now, good my lord, lie here and rest awhile.

LEAR.
Make no noise, make no noise; draw the curtains.
So, so. We'll go to supper i' the morning.

FOOL.
And I'll go to bed at noon.

Enter GLOUCESTER.

GLOUCESTER.
Come hither, friend;
Where is the King my master?

KENT.
Here, sir; but trouble him not, his wits are gone.

GLOUCESTER.
Good friend, I prythee, take him in thy arms;
I have o'erheard a plot of death upon him;
There is a litter ready; lay him in't
And drive towards Dover, friend, where thou shalt meet
Both welcome and protection. Take up thy master;
If thou shouldst dally half an hour, his life,
With thine, and all that offer to defend him,
Stand in assured loss. Take up, take up;
And follow me, that will to some provision
Give thee quick conduct.

KENT.
Oppressed nature sleeps.

This rest might yet have balm'd thy broken sinews,
Which, if convenience will not allow,
Stand in hard cure. Come, help to bear thy master;
[*To the Fool.*] Thou must not stay behind.

GLOUCESTER.
Come, come, away!

[*Exeunt* KENT, GLOUCESTER *and the* FOOL *bearing off* LEAR.]

EDGAR.
When we our betters see bearing our woes,
We scarcely think our miseries our foes.
Who alone suffers, suffers most i' the mind,
Leaving free things and happy shows behind:
But then the mind much sufferance doth o'erskip
When grief hath mates, and bearing fellowship.
How light and portable my pain seems now,
When that which makes me bend makes the King bow;
He childed as I fathered! Tom, away!
Mark the high noises; and thyself bewray,
When false opinion, whose wrong thoughts defile thee,
In thy just proof repeals and reconciles thee.
What will hap more tonight, safe 'scape the King!
Lurk, lurk.

[*Exit.*]

SCENE VII. A Room in Gloucester's Castle.

Enter CORNWALL, REGAN, GONERIL, EDMUND *and* SERVANTS.

CORNWALL.
Post speedily to my lord your husband, show him this letter: the army of France is
landed. Seek out the traitor Gloucester.

[*Exeunt some of the Servants.*]

REGAN.
Hang him instantly.

GONERIL.
Pluck out his eyes.

CORNWALL.
Leave him to my displeasure. Edmund, keep you our sister company: the revenges we
are bound to take upon your traitorous father are not fit for your beholding. Advise the
Duke where you are going, to a most festinate preparation: we are bound to the like.

Our posts shall be swift and intelligent betwixt us. Farewell, dear sister, farewell, my lord of Gloucester.

Enter OSWALD.

How now! Where's the King?

OSWALD.
My lord of Gloucester hath convey'd him hence:
Some five or six and thirty of his knights,
Hot questrists after him, met him at gate;
Who, with some other of the lord's dependants,
Are gone with him toward Dover: where they boast
To have well-armed friends.

CORNWALL.
Get horses for your mistress.

GONERIL.
Farewell, sweet lord, and sister.

CORNWALL.
Edmund, farewell.

[*Exeunt* GONERIL, EDMUND *and* OSWALD.]

Go seek the traitor Gloucester,
Pinion him like a thief, bring him before us.

[*Exeunt other Servants.*]

Though well we may not pass upon his life
Without the form of justice, yet our power
Shall do a courtesy to our wrath, which men
May blame, but not control. Who's there? The traitor?

Enter GLOUCESTER *and Servants.*

REGAN.
Ingrateful fox! 'tis he.

CORNWALL.
Bind fast his corky arms.

GLOUCESTER.
What mean your graces?
Good my friends, consider you are my guests.
Do me no foul play, friends.

CORNWALL.
Bind him, I say.

[*Servants bind him.*]

REGAN.
Hard, hard. O filthy traitor!

GLOUCESTER.
Unmerciful lady as you are, I'm none.

CORNWALL.
To this chair bind him. Villain, thou shalt find—

[REGAN *plucks his beard.*]

GLOUCESTER.
By the kind gods, 'tis most ignobly done
To pluck me by the beard.

REGAN.
So white, and such a traitor!

GLOUCESTER.
Naughty lady,
These hairs which thou dost ravish from my chin
Will quicken, and accuse thee. I am your host:
With robber's hands my hospitable favours
You should not ruffle thus. What will you do?

CORNWALL.
Come, sir, what letters had you late from France?

REGAN.
Be simple answer'd, for we know the truth.

CORNWALL.
And what confederacy have you with the traitors,
Late footed in the kingdom?

REGAN.
To whose hands have you sent the lunatic King?
Speak.

GLOUCESTER.
I have a letter guessingly set down,
Which came from one that's of a neutral heart,
And not from one oppos'd.

CORNWALL.
Cunning.

REGAN.
And false.

CORNWALL.
Where hast thou sent the King?

GLOUCESTER.
To Dover.

REGAN.
Wherefore to Dover? Wast thou not charg'd at peril,—

CORNWALL.
Wherefore to Dover? Let him first answer that.

GLOUCESTER.
I am tied to the stake, and I must stand the course.

REGAN.
Wherefore to Dover, sir?

GLOUCESTER.
Because I would not see thy cruel nails
Pluck out his poor old eyes; nor thy fierce sister
In his anointed flesh stick boarish fangs.
The sea, with such a storm as his bare head
In hell-black night endur'd, would have buoy'd up,
And quench'd the stelled fires;
Yet, poor old heart, he holp the heavens to rain.
If wolves had at thy gate howl'd that stern time,
Thou shouldst have said, 'Good porter, turn the key.'
All cruels else subscrib'd: but I shall see
The winged vengeance overtake such children.

CORNWALL.
See't shalt thou never. Fellows, hold the chair.
Upon these eyes of thine I'll set my foot.

[GLOUCESTER *is held down in his chair, while* CORNWALL *plucks out one of his eyes and sets his foot on it.*]

GLOUCESTER.
He that will think to live till he be old,
Give me some help!—O cruel! O you gods!

REGAN.
One side will mock another; the other too!

CORNWALL.
If you see vengeance—

FIRST SERVANT.
Hold your hand, my lord:
I have serv'd you ever since I was a child;
But better service have I never done you
Than now to bid you hold.

REGAN.
How now, you dog!

FIRST SERVANT.
If you did wear a beard upon your chin,
I'd shake it on this quarrel. What do you mean?

CORNWALL.
My villain?

[*Draws, and runs at him.*]

FIRST SERVANT.
Nay, then, come on, and take the chance of anger.

[*Draws. They fight.* CORNWALL *is wounded.*]

REGAN.
[*To another servant.*] Give me thy sword. A peasant stand up thus?

[*Snatches a sword, comes behind, and stabs him.*]

FIRST SERVANT.
O, I am slain! My lord, you have one eye left
To see some mischief on him. O!

[*Dies.*]

CORNWALL.
Lest it see more, prevent it. Out, vile jelly!
Where is thy lustre now?

[*Tears out* GLOUCESTER'S *other eye and throws it on the ground.*]

GLOUCESTER.
All dark and comfortless. Where's my son Edmund?
Edmund, enkindle all the sparks of nature
To quit this horrid act.

REGAN.
Out, treacherous villain!
Thou call'st on him that hates thee: it was he
That made the overture of thy treasons to us;
Who is too good to pity thee.

GLOUCESTER.
O my follies! Then Edgar was abus'd.
Kind gods, forgive me that, and prosper him!

REGAN.
Go thrust him out at gates, and let him smell
His way to Dover. How is't, my lord? How look you?

CORNWALL.
I have receiv'd a hurt: follow me, lady.
Turn out that eyeless villain. Throw this slave
Upon the dunghill. Regan, I bleed apace:
Untimely comes this hurt: give me your arm.

[*Exit* CORNWALL, *led by* REGAN; SERVANTS *unbind* GLOUCESTER *and lead him out.*]

SECOND SERVANT.
I'll never care what wickedness I do,
If this man come to good.

THIRD SERVANT.
If she live long,
And in the end meet the old course of death,
Women will all turn monsters.

SECOND SERVANT.
Let's follow the old Earl, and get the bedlam
To lead him where he would: his roguish madness
Allows itself to anything.

THIRD SERVANT.
Go thou: I'll fetch some flax and whites of eggs
To apply to his bleeding face. Now heaven help him!

[*Exeunt.*]

ACT IV

SCENE I. The heath.

Enter EDGAR.

EDGAR.
Yet better thus, and known to be contemn'd,
Than still contemn'd and flatter'd. To be worst,
The lowest and most dejected thing of fortune,
Stands still in esperance, lives not in fear:
The lamentable change is from the best;
The worst returns to laughter. Welcome then,
Thou unsubstantial air that I embrace;
The wretch that thou hast blown unto the worst
Owes nothing to thy blasts.

Enter GLOUCESTER, *led by an* OLD MAN.

But who comes here? My father, poorly led?
World, world, O world!
But that thy strange mutations make us hate thee,
Life would not yield to age.

OLD MAN.
O my good lord, I have been your tenant, and your father's tenant these fourscore
years.

GLOUCESTER.
Away, get thee away; good friend, be gone.
Thy comforts can do me no good at all;
Thee they may hurt.

OLD MAN.
You cannot see your way.

GLOUCESTER.
I have no way, and therefore want no eyes;
I stumbled when I saw. Full oft 'tis seen
Our means secure us, and our mere defects
Prove our commodities. O dear son Edgar,
The food of thy abused father's wrath!
Might I but live to see thee in my touch,
I'd say I had eyes again!

OLD MAN.
How now! Who's there?

EDGAR.
[*Aside.*] O gods! Who is't can say 'I am at the worst'?
I am worse than e'er I was.

OLD MAN.
'Tis poor mad Tom.

EDGAR.
[*Aside.*] And worse I may be yet. The worst is not
So long as we can say 'This is the worst.'

OLD MAN.
Fellow, where goest?

GLOUCESTER.
Is it a beggar-man?

OLD MAN.
Madman, and beggar too.

GLOUCESTER.
He has some reason, else he could not beg.
I' the last night's storm I such a fellow saw;
Which made me think a man a worm. My son
Came then into my mind, and yet my mind
Was then scarce friends with him.
I have heard more since.
As flies to wanton boys are we to the gods,
They kill us for their sport.

EDGAR.
[*Aside.*] How should this be?
Bad is the trade that must play fool to sorrow,
Angering itself and others. Bless thee, master!

GLOUCESTER.
Is that the naked fellow?

OLD MAN.
Ay, my lord.

GLOUCESTER.
Then prythee get thee away. If for my sake
Thou wilt o'ertake us hence a mile or twain,
I' the way toward Dover, do it for ancient love,
And bring some covering for this naked soul,
Which I'll entreat to lead me.

OLD MAN.
Alack, sir, he is mad.

GLOUCESTER.
'Tis the time's plague when madmen lead the blind.
Do as I bid thee, or rather do thy pleasure;
Above the rest, be gone.

OLD MAN.
I'll bring him the best 'parel that I have,
Come on't what will.

[*Exit.*]

GLOUCESTER.
Sirrah naked fellow.

EDGAR.
Poor Tom's a-cold.
[*Aside.*] I cannot daub it further.

GLOUCESTER.
Come hither, fellow.

EDGAR.
[*Aside.*] And yet I must. Bless thy sweet eyes, they bleed.

GLOUCESTER.
Know'st thou the way to Dover?

EDGAR.
Both stile and gate, horseway and footpath. Poor Tom hath been scared out of his
good wits. Bless thee, good man's son, from the foul fiend! Five fiends have been in
poor Tom at once; of lust, as Obidicut; Hobbididence, prince of darkness; Mahu, of
stealing; Modo, of murder; Flibbertigibbet, of mopping and mowing, who since
possesses chambermaids and waiting women. So, bless thee, master!

GLOUCESTER.
Here, take this purse, thou whom the heaven's plagues
Have humbled to all strokes: that I am wretched
Makes thee the happier. Heavens deal so still!
Let the superfluous and lust-dieted man,
That slaves your ordinance, that will not see
Because he does not feel, feel your power quickly;
So distribution should undo excess,
And each man have enough. Dost thou know Dover?

EDGAR.
Ay, master.

GLOUCESTER.
There is a cliff, whose high and bending head
Looks fearfully in the confined deep:
Bring me but to the very brim of it,
And I'll repair the misery thou dost bear
With something rich about me: from that place
I shall no leading need.

EDGAR.
Give me thy arm:
Poor Tom shall lead thee.

[*Exeunt.*]

SCENE II. Before the Duke of Albany's Palace.

Enter GONERIL, EDMUND; OSWALD *meeting them.*

GONERIL.
Welcome, my lord. I marvel our mild husband
Not met us on the way. Now, where's your master?

OSWALD.
Madam, within; but never man so chang'd.
I told him of the army that was landed;
He smil'd at it: I told him you were coming;
His answer was, 'The worse.' Of Gloucester's treachery
And of the loyal service of his son
When I inform'd him, then he call'd me sot,
And told me I had turn'd the wrong side out.
What most he should dislike seems pleasant to him;
What like, offensive.

GONERIL.
[*To Edmund.*] Then shall you go no further.
It is the cowish terror of his spirit,
That dares not undertake. He'll not feel wrongs
Which tie him to an answer. Our wishes on the way
May prove effects. Back, Edmund, to my brother;
Hasten his musters and conduct his powers.
I must change names at home, and give the distaff
Into my husband's hands. This trusty servant
Shall pass between us. Ere long you are like to hear,

If you dare venture in your own behalf,
A mistress's command. [*Giving a favour.*]
Wear this; spare speech;
Decline your head. This kiss, if it durst speak,
Would stretch thy spirits up into the air.
Conceive, and fare thee well.

EDMUND.
Yours in the ranks of death.

[*Exit* EDMUND.]

GONERIL.
My most dear Gloucester.
O, the difference of man and man!
To thee a woman's services are due;
My fool usurps my body.

OSWALD.
Madam, here comes my lord.

[*Exit.*]

   Enter ALBANY.

GONERIL.
I have been worth the whistle.

ALBANY.
O Goneril!
You are not worth the dust which the rude wind
Blows in your face! I fear your disposition;
That nature which contemns its origin
Cannot be bordered certain in itself.
She that herself will sliver and disbranch
From her material sap, perforce must wither
And come to deadly use.

GONERIL.
No more; the text is foolish.

ALBANY.
Wisdom and goodness to the vile seem vile;
Filths savour but themselves. What have you done?
Tigers, not daughters, what have you perform'd?
A father, and a gracious aged man,
Whose reverence even the head-lugg'd bear would lick,

Most barbarous, most degenerate, have you madded.
Could my good brother suffer you to do it?
A man, a prince, by him so benefitted!
If that the heavens do not their visible spirits
Send quickly down to tame these vile offences,
It will come,
Humanity must perforce prey on itself,
Like monsters of the deep.

GONERIL.
Milk-liver'd man!
That bear'st a cheek for blows, a head for wrongs;
Who hast not in thy brows an eye discerning
Thine honour from thy suffering; that not know'st
Fools do those villains pity who are punish'd
Ere they have done their mischief. Where's thy drum?
France spreads his banners in our noiseless land;
With plumed helm thy state begins to threat,
Whilst thou, a moral fool, sitt'st still, and criest
'Alack, why does he so?'

ALBANY.
See thyself, devil!
Proper deformity seems not in the fiend
So horrid as in woman.

GONERIL.
O vain fool!

ALBANY.
Thou changed and self-cover'd thing, for shame!
Be-monster not thy feature! Were't my fitness
To let these hands obey my blood.
They are apt enough to dislocate and tear
Thy flesh and bones. Howe'er thou art a fiend,
A woman's shape doth shield thee.

GONERIL.
Marry, your manhood, mew!

   Enter a MESSENGER.

ALBANY.
What news?

MESSENGER.
O, my good lord, the Duke of Cornwall's dead;
Slain by his servant, going to put out
The other eye of Gloucester.

ALBANY.
Gloucester's eyes!

MESSENGER.
A servant that he bred, thrill'd with remorse,
Oppos'd against the act, bending his sword
To his great master; who, thereat enrag'd,
Flew on him, and amongst them fell'd him dead;
But not without that harmful stroke which since
Hath pluck'd him after.

ALBANY.
This shows you are above,
You justicers, that these our nether crimes
So speedily can venge! But, O poor Gloucester!
Lost he his other eye?

MESSENGER.
Both, both, my lord.
This letter, madam, craves a speedy answer;
'Tis from your sister.

GONERIL.
[*Aside.*] One way I like this well;
But being widow, and my Gloucester with her,
May all the building in my fancy pluck
Upon my hateful life. Another way
The news is not so tart. I'll read, and answer.

[*Exit.*]

ALBANY.
Where was his son when they did take his eyes?

MESSENGER.
Come with my lady hither.

ALBANY.
He is not here.

MESSENGER.
No, my good lord; I met him back again.

ALBANY.
Knows he the wickedness?

MESSENGER.
Ay, my good lord. 'Twas he inform'd against him;
And quit the house on purpose, that their punishment
Might have the freer course.

ALBANY.
Gloucester, I live
To thank thee for the love thou show'dst the King,
And to revenge thine eyes. Come hither, friend,
Tell me what more thou know'st.

[*Exeunt.*]

SCENE III. The French camp near Dover.

Enter KENT *and a* GENTLEMAN.

KENT.
Why the King of France is so suddenly gone back, know you no reason?

GENTLEMAN.
Something he left imperfect in the state, which since his coming forth is thought of,
which imports to the kingdom so much fear and danger that his personal return was
most required and necessary.

KENT.
Who hath he left behind him general?

GENTLEMAN.
The Mareschal of France, Monsieur La Far.

KENT.
Did your letters pierce the queen to any demonstration of grief?

GENTLEMAN.
Ay, sir; she took them, read them in my presence;
And now and then an ample tear trill'd down
Her delicate cheek. It seem'd she was a queen
Over her passion; who, most rebel-like,
Sought to be king o'er her.

KENT.
O, then it mov'd her.

GENTLEMAN.
Not to a rage: patience and sorrow strove

Who should express her goodliest. You have seen
Sunshine and rain at once: her smiles and tears
Were like a better day. Those happy smilets
That play'd on her ripe lip seem'd not to know
What guests were in her eyes; which parted thence
As pearls from diamonds dropp'd. In brief,
Sorrow would be a rarity most belov'd,
If all could so become it.

KENT.
Made she no verbal question?

GENTLEMAN.
Faith, once or twice she heav'd the name of 'father'
Pantingly forth, as if it press'd her heart;
Cried 'Sisters, sisters! Shame of ladies! sisters!
Kent! father! sisters! What, i' the storm? i' the night?
Let pity not be believ'd!' There she shook
The holy water from her heavenly eyes,
And clamour master'd her: then away she started
To deal with grief alone.

KENT.
It is the stars,
The stars above us govern our conditions;
Else one self mate and make could not beget
Such different issues. You spoke not with her since?

GENTLEMAN.
No.

KENT.
Was this before the King return'd?

GENTLEMAN.
No, since.

KENT.
Well, sir, the poor distressed Lear's i' the town;
Who sometime, in his better tune, remembers
What we are come about, and by no means
Will yield to see his daughter.

GENTLEMAN.
Why, good sir?

KENT.
A sovereign shame so elbows him. His own unkindness,
That stripp'd her from his benediction, turn'd her
To foreign casualties, gave her dear rights
To his dog-hearted daughters, these things sting
His mind so venomously that burning shame
Detains him from Cordelia.

GENTLEMAN.
Alack, poor gentleman!

KENT.
Of Albany's and Cornwall's powers you heard not?

GENTLEMAN.
'Tis so; they are afoot.

KENT.
Well, sir, I'll bring you to our master Lear
And leave you to attend him. Some dear cause
Will in concealment wrap me up awhile;
When I am known aright, you shall not grieve
Lending me this acquaintance.
I pray you, go along with me.

[*Exeunt.*]

SCENE IV. The French camp. A Tent.

Enter with drum and colours, CORDELIA, PHYSICIAN *and* SOLDIERS.

CORDELIA.
Alack, 'tis he: why, he was met even now
As mad as the vex'd sea; singing aloud;
Crown'd with rank fumiter and furrow weeds,
With harlocks, hemlock, nettles, cuckoo-flowers,
Darnel, and all the idle weeds that grow
In our sustaining corn. A century send forth;
Search every acre in the high-grown field,
And bring him to our eye.

[*Exit an Officer.*]

What can man's wisdom
In the restoring his bereaved sense,
He that helps him take all my outward worth.

PHYSICIAN.
There is means, madam:
Our foster nurse of nature is repose,
The which he lacks; that to provoke in him
Are many simples operative, whose power
Will close the eye of anguish.

CORDELIA.
All bless'd secrets,
All you unpublish'd virtues of the earth,
Spring with my tears! Be aidant and remediate
In the good man's distress! Seek, seek for him;
Lest his ungovern'd rage dissolve the life
That wants the means to lead it.

Enter a MESSENGER.

MESSENGER.
News, madam;
The British powers are marching hitherward.

CORDELIA.
'Tis known before. Our preparation stands
In expectation of them. O dear father,
It is thy business that I go about;
Therefore great France
My mourning and important tears hath pitied.
No blown ambition doth our arms incite,
But love, dear love, and our ag'd father's right:
Soon may I hear and see him!

[*Exeunt.*]

SCENE V. A Room in Gloucester's Castle.

Enter REGAN *and* OSWALD.

REGAN.
But are my brother's powers set forth?

OSWALD.
Ay, madam.

REGAN.
Himself in person there?

OSWALD.
Madam, with much ado.
Your sister is the better soldier.

REGAN.
Lord Edmund spake not with your lord at home?

OSWALD.
No, madam.

REGAN.
What might import my sister's letter to him?

OSWALD.
I know not, lady.

REGAN.
Faith, he is posted hence on serious matter.
It was great ignorance, Gloucester's eyes being out,
To let him live. Where he arrives he moves
All hearts against us. Edmund, I think, is gone
In pity of his misery, to dispatch
His nighted life; moreover to descry
The strength o' th'enemy.

OSWALD.
I must needs after him, madam, with my letter.

REGAN.
Our troops set forth tomorrow; stay with us;
The ways are dangerous.

OSWALD.
I may not, madam:
My lady charg'd my duty in this business.

REGAN.
Why should she write to Edmund? Might not you
Transport her purposes by word? Belike,
Somethings, I know not what, I'll love thee much.
Let me unseal the letter.

OSWALD.
Madam, I had rather—

REGAN.
I know your lady does not love her husband;
I am sure of that; and at her late being here

She gave strange oeillades and most speaking looks
To noble Edmund. I know you are of her bosom.

OSWALD.
I, madam?

REGAN.
I speak in understanding; y'are, I know't:
Therefore I do advise you take this note:
My lord is dead; Edmund and I have talk'd,
And more convenient is he for my hand
Than for your lady's. You may gather more.
If you do find him, pray you give him this;
And when your mistress hears thus much from you,
I pray desire her call her wisdom to her.
So, fare you well.
If you do chance to hear of that blind traitor,
Preferment falls on him that cuts him off.

OSWALD.
Would I could meet him, madam! I should show
What party I do follow.

REGAN.
Fare thee well.

[*Exeunt.*]

SCENE VI. The country near Dover.

Enter GLOUCESTER, *and* EDGAR *dressed like a peasant.*

GLOUCESTER.
When shall I come to the top of that same hill?

EDGAR.
You do climb up it now. Look how we labour.

GLOUCESTER.
Methinks the ground is even.

EDGAR.
Horrible steep.
Hark, do you hear the sea?

GLOUCESTER.
No, truly.

EDGAR.
Why, then, your other senses grow imperfect
By your eyes' anguish.

GLOUCESTER.
So may it be indeed.
Methinks thy voice is alter'd; and thou speak'st
In better phrase and matter than thou didst.

EDGAR.
Y'are much deceiv'd: in nothing am I chang'd
But in my garments.

GLOUCESTER.
Methinks you're better spoken.

EDGAR.
Come on, sir; here's the place. Stand still. How fearful
And dizzy 'tis to cast one's eyes so low!
The crows and choughs that wing the midway air
Show scarce so gross as beetles. Half way down
Hangs one that gathers samphire—dreadful trade!
Methinks he seems no bigger than his head.
The fishermen that walk upon the beach
Appear like mice; and yond tall anchoring bark,
Diminish'd to her cock; her cock a buoy
Almost too small for sight: the murmuring surge
That on th'unnumber'd idle pebble chafes
Cannot be heard so high. I'll look no more;
Lest my brain turn, and the deficient sight
Topple down headlong.

GLOUCESTER.
Set me where you stand.

EDGAR.
Give me your hand.
You are now within a foot of th'extreme verge.
For all beneath the moon would I not leap upright.

GLOUCESTER.
Let go my hand.
Here, friend, 's another purse; in it a jewel
Well worth a poor man's taking. Fairies and gods
Prosper it with thee! Go thou further off;
Bid me farewell, and let me hear thee going.

EDGAR.
Now fare ye well, good sir.

[*Seems to go.*]

GLOUCESTER.
With all my heart.

EDGAR.
[*Aside.*] Why I do trifle thus with his despair
Is done to cure it.

GLOUCESTER.
O you mighty gods!
This world I do renounce, and in your sights,
Shake patiently my great affliction off:
If I could bear it longer, and not fall
To quarrel with your great opposeless wills,
My snuff and loathed part of nature should
Burn itself out. If Edgar live, O, bless him!
Now, fellow, fare thee well.

EDGAR.
Gone, sir, farewell.

[GLOUCESTER *leaps, and falls along*]

And yet I know not how conceit may rob
The treasury of life when life itself
Yields to the theft. Had he been where he thought,
By this had thought been past. Alive or dead?
Ho you, sir! friend! Hear you, sir? speak!
Thus might he pass indeed: yet he revives.
What are you, sir?

GLOUCESTER.
Away, and let me die.

EDGAR.
Hadst thou been aught but gossamer, feathers, air,
So many fathom down precipitating,
Thou'dst shiver'd like an egg: but thou dost breathe;
Hast heavy substance; bleed'st not; speak'st; art sound.
Ten masts at each make not the altitude
Which thou hast perpendicularly fell.
Thy life is a miracle. Speak yet again.

GLOUCESTER.
But have I fall'n, or no?

EDGAR.
From the dread summit of this chalky bourn.
Look up a-height, the shrill-gorg'd lark so far
Cannot be seen or heard. Do but look up.

GLOUCESTER.
Alack, I have no eyes.
Is wretchedness depriv'd that benefit
To end itself by death? 'Twas yet some comfort
When misery could beguile the tyrant's rage
And frustrate his proud will.

EDGAR.
Give me your arm.
Up, so. How is't? Feel you your legs? You stand.

GLOUCESTER.
Too well, too well.

EDGAR.
This is above all strangeness.
Upon the crown o' the cliff what thing was that
Which parted from you?

GLOUCESTER.
A poor unfortunate beggar.

EDGAR.
As I stood here below, methought his eyes
Were two full moons; he had a thousand noses,
Horns whelk'd and waved like the enraged sea.
It was some fiend. Therefore, thou happy father,
Think that the clearest gods, who make them honours
Of men's impossibilities, have preserv'd thee.

GLOUCESTER.
I do remember now: henceforth I'll bear
Affliction till it do cry out itself
'Enough, enough,' and die. That thing you speak of,
I took it for a man; often 'twould say,
'The fiend, the fiend'; he led me to that place.

EDGAR.
Bear free and patient thoughts. But who comes here?

Enter LEAR, *fantastically dressed up with flowers.*

The safer sense will ne'er accommodate
His master thus.

LEAR.
No, they cannot touch me for coining. I am the King himself.

EDGAR.
O thou side-piercing sight!

LEAR.
Nature's above art in that respect. There's your press money. That fellow handles his bow like a crow-keeper: draw me a clothier's yard. Look, look, a mouse! Peace, peace, this piece of toasted cheese will do't. There's my gauntlet; I'll prove it on a giant. Bring up the brown bills. O, well flown, bird! i' the clout, i' the clout. Hewgh! Give the word.

EDGAR.
Sweet marjoram.

LEAR.
Pass.

GLOUCESTER.
I know that voice.

LEAR.
Ha! Goneril with a white beard! They flattered me like a dog; and told me I had white hairs in my beard ere the black ones were there. To say 'ay' and 'no' to everything I said 'ay' and 'no' to was no good divinity. When the rain came to wet me once, and the wind to make me chatter; when the thunder would not peace at my bidding; there I found 'em, there I smelt 'em out. Go to, they are not men o' their words: they told me I was everything; 'tis a lie, I am not ague-proof.

GLOUCESTER.
The trick of that voice I do well remember:
Is't not the King?

LEAR.
Ay, every inch a king.
When I do stare, see how the subject quakes.
I pardon that man's life. What was thy cause?
Adultery? Thou shalt not die: die for adultery! No:
The wren goes to't, and the small gilded fly
Does lecher in my sight. Let copulation thrive;
For Gloucester's bastard son was kinder to his father

Than my daughters got 'tween the lawful sheets.
To't, luxury, pell-mell! for I lack soldiers.
Behold yond simp'ring dame,
Whose face between her forks presages snow;
That minces virtue, and does shake the head
To hear of pleasure's name.
The fitchew nor the soiled horse goes to't with a more riotous appetite. Down from the waist they are centaurs, though women all above. But to the girdle do the gods inherit, beneath is all the fiend's; there's hell, there's darkness, there is the sulphurous pit; burning, scalding, stench, consumption. Fie, fie, fie! pah, pah! Give me an ounce of civet, good apothecary, to sweeten my imagination. There's money for thee.

GLOUCESTER.
O, let me kiss that hand!

LEAR.
Let me wipe it first; it smells of mortality.

GLOUCESTER.
O ruin'd piece of nature, this great world
Shall so wear out to naught. Dost thou know me?

LEAR.
I remember thine eyes well enough. Dost thou squiny at me?
No, do thy worst, blind Cupid; I'll not love.
Read thou this challenge; mark but the penning of it.

GLOUCESTER.
Were all the letters suns, I could not see one.

EDGAR.
I would not take this from report,
It is, and my heart breaks at it.

LEAR.
Read.

GLOUCESTER.
What, with the case of eyes?

LEAR.
O, ho, are you there with me? No eyes in your head, nor no money in your purse?
Your eyes are in a heavy case, your purse in a light, yet you see how this world goes.

GLOUCESTER.
I see it feelingly.

LEAR.
What, art mad? A man may see how the world goes with no eyes. Look with thine ears. See how yon justice rails upon yon simple thief. Hark, in thine ear: change places; and, handy-dandy, which is the justice, which is the thief? Thou hast seen a farmer's dog bark at a beggar?

GLOUCESTER.
Ay, sir.

LEAR.
And the creature run from the cur? There thou mightst behold the great image of authority: a dog's obeyed in office.
Thou rascal beadle, hold thy bloody hand!
Why dost thou lash that whore? Strip thine own back;
Thou hotly lusts to use her in that kind
For which thou whipp'st her. The usurer hangs the cozener.
Through tatter'd clothes great vices do appear;
Robes and furr'd gowns hide all. Plate sin with gold,
And the strong lance of justice hurtless breaks;
Arm it in rags, a pygmy's straw does pierce it.
None does offend, none, I say none; I'll able 'em;
Take that of me, my friend, who have the power
To seal the accuser's lips. Get thee glass eyes,
And like a scurvy politician, seem
To see the things thou dost not. Now, now, now, now:
Pull off my boots: harder, harder, so.

EDGAR.
O, matter and impertinency mix'd!
Reason in madness!

LEAR.
If thou wilt weep my fortunes, take my eyes.
I know thee well enough, thy name is Gloucester.
Thou must be patient; we came crying hither:
Thou know'st the first time that we smell the air
We wawl and cry. I will preach to thee: mark.

GLOUCESTER.
Alack, alack the day!

LEAR.
When we are born, we cry that we are come
To this great stage of fools. This a good block:
It were a delicate stratagem to shoe

A troop of horse with felt. I'll put't in proof
And when I have stol'n upon these son-in-laws,
Then kill, kill, kill, kill, kill, kill!

Enter a GENTLEMAN *with Attendants.*

GENTLEMAN.
O, here he is: lay hand upon him. Sir,
Your most dear daughter—

LEAR.
No rescue? What, a prisoner? I am even
The natural fool of fortune. Use me well;
You shall have ransom. Let me have surgeons;
I am cut to the brains.

GENTLEMAN.
You shall have anything.

LEAR.
No seconds? All myself?
Why, this would make a man a man of salt,
To use his eyes for garden water-pots,
Ay, and for laying autumn's dust.

GENTLEMAN.
Good sir.

LEAR.
I will die bravely, like a smug bridegroom.
What! I will be jovial. Come, come,
I am a king, my masters, know you that.

GENTLEMAN.
You are a royal one, and we obey you.

LEAR.
Then there's life in't. Come, and you get it,
You shall get it by running. Sa, sa, sa, sa!

[*Exit running. Attendants follow.*]

GENTLEMAN.
A sight most pitiful in the meanest wretch,
Past speaking of in a king! Thou hast one daughter
Who redeems nature from the general curse
Which twain have brought her to.

EDGAR.
Hail, gentle sir.

GENTLEMAN.
Sir, speed you. What's your will?

EDGAR.
Do you hear aught, sir, of a battle toward?

GENTLEMAN.
Most sure and vulgar.
Everyone hears that, which can distinguish sound.

EDGAR.
But, by your favour,
How near's the other army?

GENTLEMAN.
Near and on speedy foot; the main descry
Stands on the hourly thought.

EDGAR.
I thank you sir, that's all.

GENTLEMAN.
Though that the queen on special cause is here,
Her army is mov'd on.

EDGAR.
I thank you, sir.

[*Exit* GENTLEMAN.]

GLOUCESTER.
You ever-gentle gods, take my breath from me;
Let not my worser spirit tempt me again
To die before you please.

EDGAR.
Well pray you, father.

GLOUCESTER.
Now, good sir, what are you?

EDGAR.
A most poor man, made tame to fortune's blows;
Who, by the art of known and feeling sorrows,
Am pregnant to good pity. Give me your hand,
I'll lead you to some biding.

GLOUCESTER.
Hearty thanks:
The bounty and the benison of heaven
To boot, and boot.

Enter OSWALD.

OSWALD.
A proclaim'd prize! Most happy!
That eyeless head of thine was first fram'd flesh
To raise my fortunes. Thou old unhappy traitor,
Briefly thyself remember. The sword is out
That must destroy thee.

GLOUCESTER.
Now let thy friendly hand
Put strength enough to't.

[EDGAR *interposes.*]

OSWALD.
Wherefore, bold peasant,
Dar'st thou support a publish'd traitor? Hence;
Lest that th'infection of his fortune take
Like hold on thee. Let go his arm.

EDGAR.
Chill not let go, zir, without vurther 'casion.

OSWALD.
Let go, slave, or thou diest!

EDGAR.
Good gentleman, go your gait, and let poor volke pass. An chud ha' bin zwaggered out of my life, 'twould not ha' bin zo long as 'tis by a vortnight. Nay, come not near th'old man; keep out, che vor ye, or ise try whether your costard or my ballow be the harder: chill be plain with you.

OSWALD.
Out, dunghill!

EDGAR.
Chill pick your teeth, zir. Come! No matter vor your foins.

[*They fight, and* EDGAR *knocks him down.*]

OSWALD.
Slave, thou hast slain me. Villain, take my purse.
If ever thou wilt thrive, bury my body;

And give the letters which thou find'st about me
To Edmund, Earl of Gloucester. Seek him out
Upon the British party. O, untimely death!

[*Dies.*]

EDGAR.
I know thee well. A serviceable villain,
As duteous to the vices of thy mistress
As badness would desire.

GLOUCESTER.
What, is he dead?

EDGAR.
Sit you down, father; rest you.
Let's see these pockets; the letters that he speaks of
May be my friends. He's dead; I am only sorry
He had no other deathsman. Let us see:
Leave, gentle wax; and, manners, blame us not.
To know our enemies' minds, we rip their hearts,
Their papers is more lawful.
[*Reads.*] 'Let our reciprocal vows be remembered. You have many opportunities to cut him off: if your will want not, time and place will be fruitfully offered. There is nothing done if he return the conqueror: then am I the prisoner, and his bed my gaol; from the loathed warmth whereof deliver me, and supply the place for your labour.
'Your (wife, so I would say) affectionate servant, 'Goneril.'
O indistinguish'd space of woman's will!
A plot upon her virtuous husband's life,
And the exchange my brother! Here in the sands
Thee I'll rake up, the post unsanctified
Of murderous lechers: and in the mature time,
With this ungracious paper strike the sight
Of the death-practis'd Duke: for him 'tis well
That of thy death and business I can tell.

[*Exit* EDGAR, *dragging out the body.*]

GLOUCESTER.
The King is mad: how stiff is my vile sense,
That I stand up, and have ingenious feeling
Of my huge sorrows! Better I were distract:
So should my thoughts be sever'd from my griefs,
And woes by wrong imaginations lose
The knowledge of themselves.

[*A drum afar off.*]

EDGAR.
Give me your hand.
Far off methinks I hear the beaten drum.
Come, father, I'll bestow you with a friend.

[*Exeunt.*]

SCENE VII. A Tent in the French Camp.

LEAR *on a bed, asleep, soft music playing;* PHYSICIAN, GENTLEMAN *and others attending.*

Enter CORDELIA *and* KENT.

CORDELIA.
O thou good Kent, how shall I live and work
To match thy goodness? My life will be too short,
And every measure fail me.

KENT.
To be acknowledg'd, madam, is o'erpaid.
All my reports go with the modest truth;
Nor more, nor clipp'd, but so.

CORDELIA.
Be better suited,
These weeds are memories of those worser hours:
I prythee put them off.

KENT.
Pardon, dear madam;
Yet to be known shortens my made intent.
My boon I make it that you know me not
Till time and I think meet.

CORDELIA.
Then be't so, my good lord. [*To the Physician.*] How, does the King?

PHYSICIAN.
Madam, sleeps still.

CORDELIA.
O you kind gods,
Cure this great breach in his abused nature!
The untun'd and jarring senses, O, wind up
Of this child-changed father.

PHYSICIAN.
So please your majesty
That we may wake the King: he hath slept long.

CORDELIA.
Be govern'd by your knowledge, and proceed
I' the sway of your own will. Is he array'd?

PHYSICIAN.
Ay, madam. In the heaviness of sleep
We put fresh garments on him.
Be by, good madam, when we do awake him;
I doubt not of his temperance.

CORDELIA.
Very well.

PHYSICIAN.
Please you draw near. Louder the music there!

CORDELIA.
O my dear father! Restoration hang
Thy medicine on my lips; and let this kiss
Repair those violent harms that my two sisters
Have in thy reverence made!

KENT.
Kind and dear princess!

CORDELIA.
Had you not been their father, these white flakes
Did challenge pity of them. Was this a face
To be oppos'd against the warring winds?
To stand against the deep dread-bolted thunder?
In the most terrible and nimble stroke
Of quick cross lightning? to watch, poor perdu!
With this thin helm? Mine enemy's dog,
Though he had bit me, should have stood that night
Against my fire; and wast thou fain, poor father,
To hovel thee with swine and rogues forlorn
In short and musty straw? Alack, alack!
'Tis wonder that thy life and wits at once
Had not concluded all. He wakes; speak to him.

PHYSICIAN.
Madam, do you; 'tis fittest.

CORDELIA.
How does my royal lord? How fares your majesty?

LEAR.
You do me wrong to take me out o' the grave.
Thou art a soul in bliss; but I am bound
Upon a wheel of fire, that mine own tears
Do scald like molten lead.

CORDELIA.
Sir, do you know me?

LEAR.
You are a spirit, I know: when did you die?

CORDELIA.
Still, still, far wide!

PHYSICIAN.
He's scarce awake: let him alone awhile.

LEAR.
Where have I been? Where am I? Fair daylight?
I am mightily abus'd. I should e'en die with pity,
To see another thus. I know not what to say.
I will not swear these are my hands: let's see;
I feel this pin prick. Would I were assur'd
Of my condition!

CORDELIA.
O, look upon me, sir,
And hold your hands in benediction o'er me.
No, sir, you must not kneel.

LEAR.
Pray, do not mock me:
I am a very foolish fond old man,
Fourscore and upward, not an hour more nor less;
And to deal plainly,
I fear I am not in my perfect mind.
Methinks I should know you, and know this man;
Yet I am doubtful: for I am mainly ignorant
What place this is; and all the skill I have
Remembers not these garments; nor I know not
Where I did lodge last night. Do not laugh at me;

For, as I am a man, I think this lady
To be my child Cordelia.

CORDELIA.
And so I am. I am.

LEAR.
Be your tears wet? Yes, faith. I pray weep not:
If you have poison for me, I will drink it.
I know you do not love me; for your sisters
Have, as I do remember, done me wrong.
You have some cause, they have not.

CORDELIA.
No cause, no cause.

LEAR.
Am I in France?

KENT.
In your own kingdom, sir.

LEAR.
Do not abuse me.

PHYSICIAN.
Be comforted, good madam, the great rage,
You see, is kill'd in him: and yet it is danger
To make him even o'er the time he has lost.
Desire him to go in; trouble him no more
Till further settling.

CORDELIA.
Will't please your highness walk?

LEAR.
You must bear with me:
Pray you now, forget and forgive: I am old and foolish.

[*Exeunt* LEAR, CORDELIA, PHYSICIAN *and Attendants.*]

GENTLEMAN.
Holds it true, sir, that the Duke of Cornwall was so slain?

KENT.
Most certain, sir.

GENTLEMAN.
Who is conductor of his people?

KENT.
As 'tis said, the bastard son of Gloucester.

GENTLEMAN.
They say Edgar, his banished son, is with the Earl of Kent in Germany.

KENT.
Report is changeable. 'Tis time to look about; the powers of the kingdom approach
apace.

GENTLEMAN.
The arbitrement is like to be bloody.
Fare you well, sir.

[*Exit.*]

KENT.
My point and period will be throughly wrought,
Or well or ill, as this day's battle's fought.

[*Exit.*]

ACT V

SCENE I. The Camp of the British Forces near Dover.

Enter, with drum and colours EDMUND, REGAN, OFFICERS, SOLDIERS *and others.*

EDMUND.
Know of the Duke if his last purpose hold,
Or whether since he is advis'd by aught
To change the course, he's full of alteration
And self-reproving, bring his constant pleasure.

[*To an Officer, who goes out.*]

REGAN.
Our sister's man is certainly miscarried.

EDMUND.
'Tis to be doubted, madam.

REGAN.
Now, sweet lord,
You know the goodness I intend upon you:

Tell me but truly, but then speak the truth,
Do you not love my sister?

EDMUND.
In honour'd love.

REGAN.
But have you never found my brother's way
To the forfended place?

EDMUND.
That thought abuses you.

REGAN.
I am doubtful that you have been conjunct
And bosom'd with her, as far as we call hers.

EDMUND.
No, by mine honour, madam.

REGAN.
I never shall endure her, dear my lord,
Be not familiar with her.

EDMUND.
Fear not,
She and the Duke her husband!

Enter with drum and colours ALBANY, GONERIL *and* SOLDIERS.

GONERIL.
[*Aside.*] I had rather lose the battle than that sister
Should loosen him and me.

ALBANY.
Our very loving sister, well be-met.
Sir, this I heard: the King is come to his daughter,
With others whom the rigour of our state
Forc'd to cry out. Where I could not be honest,
I never yet was valiant. For this business,
It toucheth us as France invades our land,
Not bolds the King, with others whom I fear
Most just and heavy causes make oppose.

EDMUND.
Sir, you speak nobly.

REGAN.
Why is this reason'd?

GONERIL.
Combine together 'gainst the enemy;
For these domestic and particular broils
Are not the question here.

ALBANY.
Let's, then, determine with the ancient of war
On our proceeding.

EDMUND.
I shall attend you presently at your tent.

REGAN.
Sister, you'll go with us?

GONERIL.
No.

REGAN.
'Tis most convenient; pray you, go with us.

GONERIL.
[*Aside*.] O, ho, I know the riddle. I will go.

[*Exeunt* EDMUND, REGAN, GONERIL, OFFICERS, SOLDIERS *and* ATTENDANTS.]

As they are going out, enter EDGAR *disguised.*

EDGAR.
If e'er your grace had speech with man so poor,
Hear me one word.

ALBANY.
I'll overtake you. Speak.

EDGAR.
Before you fight the battle, ope this letter.
If you have victory, let the trumpet sound
For him that brought it: wretched though I seem,
I can produce a champion that will prove
What is avouched there. If you miscarry,
Your business of the world hath so an end,
And machination ceases. Fortune love you!

ALBANY.
Stay till I have read the letter.

EDGAR.
I was forbid it.

When time shall serve, let but the herald cry,
And I'll appear again.

ALBANY.
Why, fare thee well. I will o'erlook thy paper.

[*Exit* EDGAR.]

Enter EDMUND.

EDMUND.
The enemy's in view; draw up your powers.
Here is the guess of their true strength and forces
By diligent discovery; but your haste
Is now urg'd on you.

ALBANY.
We will greet the time.

[*Exit.*]

EDMUND.
To both these sisters have I sworn my love;
Each jealous of the other, as the stung
Are of the adder. Which of them shall I take?
Both? One? Or neither? Neither can be enjoy'd,
If both remain alive. To take the widow
Exasperates, makes mad her sister Goneril;
And hardly shall I carry out my side,
Her husband being alive. Now, then, we'll use
His countenance for the battle; which being done,
Let her who would be rid of him devise
His speedy taking off. As for the mercy
Which he intends to Lear and to Cordelia,
The battle done, and they within our power,
Shall never see his pardon: for my state
Stands on me to defend, not to debate.

[*Exit.*]

SCENE II. A field between the two Camps.

Alarum within. Enter with drum and colours, LEAR, CORDELIA *and their Forces,
and exeunt.*

Enter EDGAR *and* GLOUCESTER.

EDGAR.
Here, father, take the shadow of this tree
For your good host; pray that the right may thrive:
If ever I return to you again,
I'll bring you comfort.

GLOUCESTER.
Grace go with you, sir!

[*Exit* EDGAR.]

   Alarum and retreat within. Enter EDGAR.

EDGAR.
Away, old man, give me thy hand, away!
King Lear hath lost, he and his daughter ta'en:
Give me thy hand; come on!

GLOUCESTER.
No further, sir; a man may rot even here.

EDGAR.
What, in ill thoughts again? Men must endure
Their going hence, even as their coming hither;
Ripeness is all. Come on.

GLOUCESTER.
And that's true too.

[*Exeunt.*]

SCENE III. The British Camp near Dover.

Enter in conquest with drum and colours, EDMUND, LEAR *and* CORDELIA *as prisoners; Officers, Soldiers, &c.*

EDMUND.
Some officers take them away: good guard
Until their greater pleasures first be known
That are to censure them.

CORDELIA.
We are not the first
Who with best meaning have incurr'd the worst.
For thee, oppressed King, I am cast down;
Myself could else out-frown false fortune's frown.
Shall we not see these daughters and these sisters?

LEAR.

No, no, no, no. Come, let's away to prison:
We two alone will sing like birds i' the cage:
When thou dost ask me blessing I'll kneel down
And ask of thee forgiveness. So we'll live,
And pray, and sing, and tell old tales, and laugh
At gilded butterflies, and hear poor rogues
Talk of court news; and we'll talk with them too,
Who loses and who wins; who's in, who's out;
And take upon's the mystery of things,
As if we were God's spies. And we'll wear out,
In a wall'd prison, packs and sects of great ones
That ebb and flow by the moon.

EDMUND.

Take them away.

LEAR.

Upon such sacrifices, my Cordelia,
The gods themselves throw incense. Have I caught thee?
He that parts us shall bring a brand from heaven,
And fire us hence like foxes. Wipe thine eyes;
The good years shall devour them, flesh and fell,
Ere they shall make us weep!
We'll see 'em starve first: come.

[*Exeunt* LEAR *and* CORDELIA, *guarded.*]

EDMUND.

Come hither, captain, hark.
Take thou this note [*giving a paper*]; go follow them to prison.
One step I have advanc'd thee; if thou dost
As this instructs thee, thou dost make thy way
To noble fortunes: know thou this, that men
Are as the time is; to be tender-minded
Does not become a sword. Thy great employment
Will not bear question; either say thou'lt do't,
Or thrive by other means.

CAPTAIN.

I'll do't, my lord.

EDMUND.

About it; and write happy when thou hast done.

Mark, I say, instantly; and carry it so
As I have set it down.

CAPTAIN.
I cannot draw a cart, nor eat dried oats;
If it be man's work, I'll do't.

[*Exit.*]

Flourish. Enter ALBANY, GONERIL, REGAN, OFFICERS *and* ATTENDANTS.

ALBANY.
Sir, you have show'd today your valiant strain,
And fortune led you well: you have the captives
Who were the opposites of this day's strife:
I do require them of you, so to use them
As we shall find their merits and our safety
May equally determine.

EDMUND.
Sir, I thought it fit
To send the old and miserable King
To some retention and appointed guard;
Whose age has charms in it, whose title more,
To pluck the common bosom on his side,
And turn our impress'd lances in our eyes
Which do command them. With him I sent the queen;
My reason all the same; and they are ready
Tomorrow, or at further space, to appear
Where you shall hold your session. At this time
We sweat and bleed: the friend hath lost his friend;
And the best quarrels in the heat are curs'd
By those that feel their sharpness.
The question of Cordelia and her father
Requires a fitter place.

ALBANY.
Sir, by your patience,
I hold you but a subject of this war,
Not as a brother.

REGAN.
That's as we list to grace him.
Methinks our pleasure might have been demanded
Ere you had spoke so far. He led our powers;
Bore the commission of my place and person;

The which immediacy may well stand up
And call itself your brother.

GONERIL.
Not so hot:
In his own grace he doth exalt himself,
More than in your addition.

REGAN.
In my rights,
By me invested, he compeers the best.

ALBANY.
That were the most, if he should husband you.

REGAN.
Jesters do oft prove prophets.

GONERIL.
Holla, holla!
That eye that told you so look'd but asquint.

REGAN.
Lady, I am not well; else I should answer
From a full-flowing stomach. General,
Take thou my soldiers, prisoners, patrimony;
Dispose of them, of me; the walls are thine:
Witness the world that I create thee here
My lord and master.

GONERIL.
Mean you to enjoy him?

ALBANY.
The let-alone lies not in your good will.

EDMUND.
Nor in thine, lord.

ALBANY.
Half-blooded fellow, yes.

REGAN.
[*To Edmund.*] Let the drum strike, and prove my title thine.

ALBANY.
Stay yet; hear reason: Edmund, I arrest thee
On capital treason; and, in thine arrest,
This gilded serpent. [*pointing to Goneril.*]

For your claim, fair sister,
I bar it in the interest of my wife;
'Tis she is sub-contracted to this lord,
And I her husband contradict your bans.
If you will marry, make your loves to me,
My lady is bespoke.

GONERIL.
An interlude!

ALBANY.
Thou art arm'd, Gloucester. Let the trumpet sound:
If none appear to prove upon thy person
Thy heinous, manifest, and many treasons,
There is my pledge. [*Throwing down a glove.*]
I'll make it on thy heart,
Ere I taste bread, thou art in nothing less
Than I have here proclaim'd thee.

REGAN.
Sick, O, sick!

GONERIL.
[*Aside.*] If not, I'll ne'er trust medicine.

EDMUND.
There's my exchange. [*Throwing down a glove.*]
What in the world he is
That names me traitor, villain-like he lies.
Call by thy trumpet: he that dares approach,
On him, on you, who not? I will maintain
My truth and honour firmly.

ALBANY.
A herald, ho!

   Enter a HERALD.

Trust to thy single virtue; for thy soldiers,
All levied in my name, have in my name
Took their discharge.

REGAN.
My sickness grows upon me.

ALBANY.
She is not well. Convey her to my tent.

[*Exit* REGAN, *led.*]

Come hither, herald. Let the trumpet sound
And read out this.

OFFICER.
Sound, trumpet!

[*A trumpet sounds.*]

HERALD.
[*Reads.*] 'If any man of quality or degree within the lists of the army will maintain upon Edmund, supposed Earl of Gloucester, that he is a manifold traitor, let him appear by the third sound of the trumpet. He is bold in his defence.'

EDMUND.
Sound!

[*First trumpet.*]

HERALD.
Again!

[*Second trumpet.*]

HERALD.
Again!

Third trumpet. Trumpet answers within. Enter EDGAR, *armed, preceded by a trumpet.*

ALBANY.
Ask him his purposes, why he appears
Upon this call o' the trumpet.

HERALD.
What are you?
Your name, your quality? and why you answer
This present summons?

EDGAR.
Know my name is lost;
By treason's tooth bare-gnawn and canker-bit.
Yet am I noble as the adversary
I come to cope.

ALBANY.
Which is that adversary?

EDGAR.
What's he that speaks for Edmund, Earl of Gloucester?

EDMUND.
Himself, what say'st thou to him?

EDGAR.
Draw thy sword,
That if my speech offend a noble heart,
Thy arm may do thee justice: here is mine.
Behold, it is the privilege of mine honours,
My oath, and my profession: I protest,
Maugre thy strength, youth, place, and eminence,
Despite thy victor sword and fire-new fortune,
Thy valour and thy heart, thou art a traitor;
False to thy gods, thy brother, and thy father;
Conspirant 'gainst this high illustrious prince;
And, from the extremest upward of thy head
To the descent and dust beneath thy foot,
A most toad-spotted traitor. Say thou 'No,'
This sword, this arm, and my best spirits are bent
To prove upon thy heart, whereto I speak,
Thou liest.

EDMUND.
In wisdom I should ask thy name;
But since thy outside looks so fair and warlike,
And that thy tongue some say of breeding breathes,
What safe and nicely I might well delay
By rule of knighthood, I disdain and spurn.
Back do I toss those treasons to thy head,
With the hell-hated lie o'erwhelm thy heart;
Which for they yet glance by and scarcely bruise,
This sword of mine shall give them instant way,
Where they shall rest for ever. Trumpets, speak!

[*Alarums. They fight.* EDMUND *falls.*]

ALBANY.
Save him, save him!

GONERIL.
This is mere practice, Gloucester:
By the law of arms thou wast not bound to answer

An unknown opposite; thou art not vanquish'd,
But cozen'd and beguil'd.

ALBANY.
Shut your mouth, dame,
Or with this paper shall I stop it. Hold, sir;
Thou worse than any name, read thine own evil.
No tearing, lady; I perceive you know it.

[*Gives the letter to* EDMUND.]

GONERIL.
Say if I do, the laws are mine, not thine:
Who can arraign me for't?

[*Exit.*]

ALBANY.
Most monstrous! O!
Know'st thou this paper?

EDMUND.
Ask me not what I know.

ALBANY.
[*To an Officer, who goes out.*] Go after her; she's desperate; govern her.

EDMUND.
What you have charg'd me with, that have I done;
And more, much more; the time will bring it out.
'Tis past, and so am I. But what art thou
That hast this fortune on me? If thou'rt noble,
I do forgive thee.

EDGAR.
Let's exchange charity.
I am no less in blood than thou art, Edmund;
If more, the more thou hast wrong'd me.
My name is Edgar and thy father's son.
The gods are just, and of our pleasant vices
Make instruments to plague us:
The dark and vicious place where thee he got
Cost him his eyes.

EDMUND.
Thou hast spoken right, 'tis true;
The wheel is come full circle; I am here.

ALBANY.
Methought thy very gait did prophesy
A royal nobleness. I must embrace thee.
Let sorrow split my heart if ever I
Did hate thee or thy father.

EDGAR.
Worthy prince, I know't.

ALBANY.
Where have you hid yourself?
How have you known the miseries of your father?

EDGAR.
By nursing them, my lord. List a brief tale;
And when 'tis told, O that my heart would burst!
The bloody proclamation to escape
That follow'd me so near,—O, our lives' sweetness!
That with the pain of death we'd hourly die
Rather than die at once!—taught me to shift
Into a madman's rags; t'assume a semblance
That very dogs disdain'd; and in this habit
Met I my father with his bleeding rings,
Their precious stones new lost; became his guide,
Led him, begg'd for him, sav'd him from despair;
Never,—O fault!—reveal'd myself unto him
Until some half hour past, when I was arm'd;
Not sure, though hoping of this good success,
I ask'd his blessing, and from first to last
Told him my pilgrimage. But his flaw'd heart,
Alack, too weak the conflict to support!
'Twixt two extremes of passion, joy and grief,
Burst smilingly.

EDMUND.
This speech of yours hath mov'd me,
And shall perchance do good, but speak you on;
You look as you had something more to say.

ALBANY.
If there be more, more woeful, hold it in;
For I am almost ready to dissolve,
Hearing of this.

EDGAR.
This would have seem'd a period
To such as love not sorrow; but another,
To amplify too much, would make much more,
And top extremity.
Whilst I was big in clamour, came there a man
Who, having seen me in my worst estate,
Shunn'd my abhorr'd society; but then finding
Who 'twas that so endur'd, with his strong arms
He fastened on my neck, and bellow'd out
As he'd burst heaven; threw him on my father;
Told the most piteous tale of Lear and him
That ever ear receiv'd, which in recounting
His grief grew puissant, and the strings of life
Began to crack. Twice then the trumpets sounded,
And there I left him tranc'd.

ALBANY.
But who was this?

EDGAR.
Kent, sir, the banish'd Kent; who in disguise
Follow'd his enemy king and did him service
Improper for a slave.

    Enter a GENTLEMAN *hastily, with a bloody knife.*

GENTLEMAN.
Help, help! O, help!

EDGAR.
What kind of help?

ALBANY.
Speak, man.

EDGAR.
What means this bloody knife?

GENTLEMAN.
'Tis hot, it smokes;
It came even from the heart of—O! she's dead!

ALBANY.
Who dead? Speak, man.

GENTLEMAN.
Your lady, sir, your lady; and her sister
By her is poisoned; she hath confesses it.

EDMUND.
I was contracted to them both, all three
Now marry in an instant.

EDGAR.
Here comes Kent.

    Enter KENT.

ALBANY.
Produce their bodies, be they alive or dead.
This judgement of the heavens that makes us tremble
Touches us not with pity. O, is this he?
The time will not allow the compliment
Which very manners urges.

KENT.
I am come
To bid my King and master aye good night:
Is he not here?

ALBANY.
Great thing of us forgot!
Speak, Edmund, where's the King? and where's Cordelia?

    The bodies of GONERIL *and* REGAN *are brought in.*

Seest thou this object, Kent?

KENT.
Alack, why thus?

EDMUND.
Yet Edmund was belov'd.
The one the other poisoned for my sake,
And after slew herself.

ALBANY.
Even so. Cover their faces.

EDMUND.
I pant for life. Some good I mean to do,
Despite of mine own nature. Quickly send,
Be brief in it, to the castle; for my writ

Is on the life of Lear and on Cordelia;
Nay, send in time.

ALBANY.
Run, run, O, run!

EDGAR.
To who, my lord? Who has the office? Send
Thy token of reprieve.

EDMUND.
Well thought on: take my sword,
Give it the captain.

EDGAR.
Haste thee for thy life.

[*Exit* EDGAR.]

EDMUND.
He hath commission from thy wife and me
To hang Cordelia in the prison, and
To lay the blame upon her own despair,
That she fordid herself.

ALBANY.
The gods defend her! Bear him hence awhile.

[EDMUND *is borne off.*]

   Enter LEAR *with* CORDELIA *dead in his arms;* EDGAR, OFFICER *and others*
   following.

LEAR.
Howl, howl, howl, howl! O, you are men of stone.
Had I your tongues and eyes, I'ld use them so
That heaven's vault should crack. She's gone for ever!
I know when one is dead, and when one lives;
She's dead as earth. Lend me a looking glass;
If that her breath will mist or stain the stone,
Why, then she lives.

KENT.
Is this the promis'd end?

EDGAR.
Or image of that horror?

ALBANY.
Fall, and cease!

LEAR.
This feather stirs; she lives! If it be so,
It is a chance which does redeem all sorrows
That ever I have felt.

KENT.
O, my good master! [*Kneeling.*]

LEAR.
Prythee, away!

EDGAR.
'Tis noble Kent, your friend.

LEAR.
A plague upon you, murderers, traitors all!
I might have sav'd her; now she's gone for ever!
Cordelia, Cordelia! stay a little. Ha!
What is't thou say'st? Her voice was ever soft,
Gentle, and low, an excellent thing in woman.
I kill'd the slave that was a-hanging thee.

OFFICER.
'Tis true, my lords, he did.

LEAR.
Did I not, fellow?
I have seen the day, with my good biting falchion
I would have made them skip. I am old now,
And these same crosses spoil me. Who are you?
Mine eyes are not o' the best, I'll tell you straight.

KENT.
If Fortune brag of two she lov'd and hated,
One of them we behold.

LEAR.
This is a dull sight. Are you not Kent?

KENT.
The same,
Your servant Kent. Where is your servant Caius?

LEAR.
He's a good fellow, I can tell you that;
He'll strike, and quickly too:. He's dead and rotten.

KENT.
No, my good lord; I am the very man.

LEAR.
I'll see that straight.

KENT.
That from your first of difference and decay
Have follow'd your sad steps.

LEAR.
You are welcome hither.

KENT.
Nor no man else. All's cheerless, dark and deadly.
Your eldest daughters have fordone themselves,
And desperately are dead.

LEAR.
Ay, so I think.

ALBANY.
He knows not what he says; and vain is it
That we present us to him.

EDGAR.
Very bootless.

   Enter an OFFICER.

OFFICER.
Edmund is dead, my lord.

ALBANY.
That's but a trifle here.
You lords and noble friends, know our intent.
What comfort to this great decay may come
Shall be applied For us, we will resign,
During the life of this old majesty,
To him our absolute power;
[*to Edgar and Kent*] you to your rights;
With boot and such addition as your honours
Have more than merited. All friends shall taste

The wages of their virtue and all foes
The cup of their deservings. O, see, see!

LEAR.
And my poor fool is hang'd! No, no, no life!
Why should a dog, a horse, a rat have life,
And thou no breath at all? Thou'lt come no more,
Never, never, never, never, never!
Pray you undo this button. Thank you, sir.
Do you see this? Look on her: look, her lips,
Look there, look there!

[*He dies.*]

EDGAR.
He faints! My lord, my lord!

KENT.
Break, heart; I prythee break!

EDGAR.
Look up, my lord.

KENT.
Vex not his ghost: O, let him pass! He hates him
That would upon the rack of this rough world
Stretch him out longer.

EDGAR.
He is gone indeed.

KENT.
The wonder is, he hath endur'd so long:
He but usurp'd his life.

ALBANY.
Bear them from hence. Our present business
Is general woe. [*To Edgar and Kent.*] Friends of my soul, you twain,
Rule in this realm and the gor'd state sustain.

KENT.
I have a journey, sir, shortly to go;
My master calls me, I must not say no.

EDGAR.
The weight of this sad time we must obey;
Speak what we feel, not what we ought to say.

The oldest hath borne most; we that are young
Shall never see so much, nor live so long.

[*Exeunt with a dead march.*]

Made in the USA
Las Vegas, NV
30 December 2021

39841494R00070